THE GOD THAT YOU ARE

'The fully realized man'

Martin Guinness

Lifedancer Publishing

Copyright © 2018 Martin Guinness

The right of Martin Guinness to be identified as the author of this work has been asserted by him

All rights reserved. No part of this book may be used or reproduced in any manner whatsoever without written permission from the Publisher except in the case of brief quotations embodied in critical articles or reviews.

Lifedancer Publishing

Sydney, Australia

lifedancer.publish@gmail.com

ISBN 978-0-646-97720-1

Typeset by Lifedancer Publishing

www.lifedancerpublishing.com

INTRODUCTION

Being a god is about being the best that *you* can be. Not better than anyone else, but fully empowering yourself.

This book came about after an interaction that I had with someone very close to me, and the thought came to me as clear as daylight: "Just because I'm showing you my human face doesn't mean I am not a god".

This is not an entirely new concept. The Sanskrit word "brahmacharya" (from the ancient Vedas and early Upanishadic texts of Hinduism) literally means "living as a god" – living a life divine. And in Genesis 1:27 it says "So God created man in his own image, in the image of God created he him; male and female created he them".

We were all born gods. But most of us have either forgotten how to live as gods or were discouraged from doing so. There are men who are already familiar with many of the principles discussed here. However, it is also quite likely that they often forget them. In any event, it would certainly be useful to see them in a new context.

Many men seem to live their lives as though they are driving their car in first gear, with the handbrake on, using only some of the motor's cylinders, towing a trailer full of baggage. And looking around them to see what other people think of them. You don't have to live your life anything like this. You were born as a god and you can continue to live as a god, regardless of your circumstances.

This is your opportunity to free yourself, stop sleepwalking, and be who you truly are. When you have read this book you will not only see for yourself how it feels to be a god, you will be able to tune into yourself perfectly. You can learn how to harness your own thoughts and emotions, and create your own destiny. This is how you can transform your life.

Although this book is directed towards men and boys, women and girls may also gain some insight from these words. However, for some time now, women have been learning how to be goddesses, and too little has been written specifically for men on this subject.

Embracing your god-ness is about maturing a man. And it is the ultimate way in which a man can live.

What kind of god could you be? That is entirely up to you. There are as many types of gods on this planet as there are people because, obviously, each of us is unique. There is no template that you have to fit, nor do you have to adhere to someone else's idea of what a god is.

I hope you enjoy this voyage of self-discovery.

CONTENTS

1: WHAT DO YOU MEAN "I'M A GOD"? 1
2: WHAT IS THE DIFFERENCE BETWEEN A GOD AND AN ORDINARY MAN? 7
3: THE QUALITIES THAT A GOD POSSESSES 13
    Dignity 13
    Love 15
    Awareness & Consciousness 18
    Integrity 31
    Authenticity 33
    Honour 42
    Compassion 43
    Grace 44
    Trust 48
4: IS BEING A GOD THE SAME AS BEING A WARRIOR? 51
5: ON BEING A GOD (WALKING, TALKING, BEING) 59
6: HOW DO YOU TREAT YOUR BODY, YOUR MIND, AND YOUR EMOTIONS 71
7: REALIZING YOUR FULL POTENTIAL 91
8: ACCEPT YOURSELF, ACCEPT YOURSELF, ACCEPT YOURSELF 101
9: THE GOD AND HIS GODDESS 111
10: HOW CAN I BELIEVE THAT I AM A GOD 121
11: REMEMBERING THAT I'M A GOD 127
12: GETTING CLEAR IN YOURSELF AND ABOUT YOURSELF 135
13: IMPROVING YOUR SKILL SET 147
14: HEALING YOURSELF 153

15: FINDING YOUR CENTRE AGAIN IF YOU LOSE IT 161
16: TEACH YOUR SONS TO BE GODS 165
17: LIVE AS A GOD 177
APPENDIX 189
   A little exercise to practise projecting your energy: 189
   The 'light bulb' meditation: 190
   The tense-relax exercise: 191

1: WHAT DO YOU MEAN "I'M A GOD"?

> **'A god owns who he is.**
> **Everything about who he is'**

Aside from religious figures, is there a man, living or dead, whom you would describe as a god? If you had to nominate a man whom you could say you think is a god, who would you point to? A sportsman, a film actor, a singer? Why? What qualities does this man possess? And what is it that you think this man might have that you don't?

My message to you is simple, and it is this: You are a god. The reaction from the majority of men is "No I'm not". Often they will say this automatically without even thinking about it. And that's because they have a fixed idea of what the statement "I am a god" means. Try it for yourself – say, out loud, "I am a god". For many it feels incredibly awkward. Or just plain wrong.

So, let's get clear what kind of god we're talking about? Firstly I'm not suggesting that you are 'God'. Not the creator and ruler of the universe and source of all moral authority. The supreme being. The Big Man in the Sky. There are institutions for people who claim to be "God". Although there is an argument to be made that there is a little bit of God in all of us. Or, even, that we all together constitute God. But I'm not talking about that.

Do I mean that you have superhuman or supernatural powers? No. Are you a being or spirit to be worshipped as having power over nature or human fortunes? Well, maybe. But only worshipped by yourself. Although that doesn't mean that others can't recognize you as a god.

No, the 'god' I'm talking about here is a fully realized man. He doesn't look to others to validate him, and he isn't perturbed by others' thoughts about him either. A god believes in himself. And you can too. It doesn't matter what anyone else thinks or says. Let me repeat that: It doesn't matter what anyone else thinks or says. It's not necessary for others to regard you as a god. It's how you regard yourself. You were born a god and you remain a god. Even if you can't see it yourself.

Ernest Hemingway wrote "There is nothing noble in being superior to your fellow man; true nobility is being superior to your former self." You can be superior to your former self by fully realizing yourself as a god.

But why call yourself a 'god'? Couldn't you just be a fully-realized man? No, because that's not enough. That's like describing a champion racehorse as "a horse". Obviously it is a horse, but it's so much more than that, just as you are more than just "a man". You could, of course, just be a man, but then you would be missing a part of yourself. (I'll explain how and why in later chapters.) And I believe that each of us is obliged to be the most that we can be in life. And this means embodying the gods that we are.

Yes, 'god' is an emotive word. And that's the point! Maybe using the word will shock you into becoming your true self. Because, since you were a baby, you have probably been moving away from your true self. Now it's time to come back home. To come back home to you.

THE GOD THAT YOU ARE

And, let's be clear: I'm not saying you could be a god. I'm not saying that, with enough practise, you might become a god. I'm saying that you already are a god. You may not be realized or embody that god-ness yet. But you're already a god. You just need to see it and acknowledge it.

Why would anyone want to be a god? Here are a couple of very good reasons:

Because it's your destiny (it was what you were born to be),

Because I believe that it will make you happier! That is, you will feel more fulfilled and more satisfied with life. Isn't that a good reason to embrace being a god? Of course it is!

In the meantime your relationships will improve and you'll be healthier. I can't promise that you'll become richer, but you never know! Understanding that you are a god also gives you confidence and is better for you socially.

"Okay", you might say, "I'm not "God". But I'm a god, What special powers do I have then?".

Here's the thing: the one special power that you already have is the only one you'll ever really need: the power over yourself. And it's important to see that you do already have that power (and later on we'll be talking about how you can access that power).

So, what precisely do we mean when we talk about a 'god'? And what is the distinction between a god and an ordinary man?

Let's just pause for a moment. Can you accept that it's actually possible to be a god? Is your mind open to that possibility? If you can accept that possibility – even just a little – well, good.

Do you realize that every time you act you give yourself permission to take that action. Similarly, every time you make a decision, you give yourself permission to make that decision? This includes simple, basic activities like standing up from a chair, as well as major decisions like moving to another country. In between, in every moment of your life, you are giving yourself permission. And that includes accepting ideas. Not that there's often much of a debate about it. We generally give ourselves permission in a subconscious (or unconscious) way. Therefore I propose that you give yourself permission to acknowledge that you are a god.

Now, if you have accepted that it's actually possible to be a god, can you see that you might evolve into your god-self? Can you embrace that concept? And does anything come to your mind as to how that evolution might take place? What do you think is the difference between how you are currently as you read this and how you might become? What qualities might you have as a god that you, currently don't own?

How does a god live differently to how most men live? Here are a few ways:

A god fully inhabits himself.

He is awake to all of his potential.

He is alive to all the possibilities that life has to offer him.

His mind is tuned and he is fully aware and conscious of the world immediately around him.

He understands himself – his motives, his drives, his needs. And he is constantly growing in this knowledge.

He rises to challenges.

He is dedicated to furthering his growth and the growth of the world around him.

A god owns who he is. *Everything* about who he is! He owns his abilities, his triumphs, his talents, his magnificence. And he also owns his dark side, his 'failures', his ineptness in certain areas, and all the areas to which he especially needs to pay attention. (I have been asked how a god can 'fail' or has a dark side. "Aren't these very human qualities?" Well, yes and no. I will go into this in

THE GOD THAT YOU ARE

greater detail later. But, for the time being, suffice it to say that what I'm talking about here is awareness and ownership.)

A god is acutely aware of where his energy ends and the rest of the world begins. Note that we're not just talking about where his body ends. Because a god's energy extends way beyond his physical body. Have you noticed in social situations that eyes are drawn to certain men? And, in the same situations, that other men become virtually invisible. A major reason for this phenomenon is the projection (or otherwise) of the man's energy. At the end of this book is a little exercise to practice projecting your energy.

If this figure represents a god

(or the complete man).....

.....then this figure represents

man as he often is

(in other words, incomplete)

I urge you to be the complete man: the all-that-you-can-be man

Someone said to me recently "You have a sense of entitlement" as though there was something wrong with that. Well, yes, I understood what they meant: that I was being selfish in that moment. And that I was not considering others. That may or may not have been true in that moment. However, while being conscious of, and compassionate for, others it is still possible to have a sense of entitlement. I'm entitled to stand up for myself. I'm entitled to assert my rights. I'm entitled to claim what is rightfully mine. In the process I'm not claiming something that belongs to others. I'm accepting what the universe is offering me. So, yes, I have a sense of entitlement.

2: WHAT IS THE DIFFERENCE BETWEEN A GOD AND AN ORDINARY MAN?

> **'Seek the purest form of *you*.**
>
> **Then you will arrive at your Higher Self'**

One way to understand the difference between a god and an ordinary man is by thinking about the difference between a man who just likes playing sport and an elite sportsman. They might both train and learn techniques and live a healthy and balanced life. But the elite sportsman takes matters to a much higher level. His training is more sophisticated, more rigorous and more frequent. The techniques he learns are more advanced. And his focus on health is more thorough. As a result there is a certain, almost indefinable zone that he enters which raises him up to the higher level.

Like a finely-tuned machine, a god is completely in touch with himself, with what is happening around him, and with his feelings. And, even while expressing an emotion he observes that, at that moment, he's not just angry or joyous. He *is* anger, or joy. He is in tune with his body, and can feel the energy of every part of himself. And he is also aware of his mental state. He does everything with awareness. Even if he is going to get drunk he does it consciously and he understands why he is doing it. And you can do the same. It just takes practise.

Of course, one of the fundamental differences between an ordinary man and a god is that a god at least considers the possibility that he is a god. He aspires to, and is willing to put effort into, embodying his god-ness. An ordinary man, on the other hand, simply doesn't care. He will remain stuck at a particular level. And, of course, this is fine for so many men. There will be some happiness in their lives and there will be other rewards. But they will never know what it feels like to be a god. And they will be missing out big time.

Where to locate the god-ness particle

A man is made up of many parts and plays many roles. He may be son, father, grandfather, brother, lover, friend, employee, employer, team member, comrade. He may also be deeply identified with other aspects of himself, whether that's sport or another activity of some kind, a religious or political group. Many men believe that these are the elements which define who they are. But there is something else which they often discount or have never even thought about. This is their Higher Self. And it's the understanding and integration of this Higher Self which defines whether a man remains just a man or becomes a god.

So, what exactly is your Higher Self? More than anything, it's a state of being which you enter and inhabit when you rise above the mundane. (Here 'mundane' can be defined as relating to the earthly world rather than a spiritual world).

It is the purest essence of who you are and best that you can be....and then just a little bit more. Which is why an elite sportsman never really competes against others. He competes against his own Personal Best. And, by pursuing your own Personal Best, you will begin to find that god-ness particle.

Where do you find the discipline that is necessary to integrate your Higher Self? It's like anything else: a muscle – or a group of muscles – which you use regularly. In this case you find the discipline in your desire, your determination, your application, and your own wisdom. I imagine, if you've got to this part of the book, you must be at least, to a certain extent, interested in embracing your god-ness. If you follow the guidelines that I've laid out in this book then you will find the way.

Seek the purest form of you. Then you will arrive at your Higher Self. And you will see your god-ness for yourself. It will become so obvious to you at that time.

How to identify the purest form of you

I'll bet there are many times in your life when you know that you're only doing half a job, when you're not really committed to the task in hand. 'Close enough is good enough'. is often the rule under which we live. And that's often how some men live their whole lives. They'll put in the least amount of effort to extract the maximum benefit, whether that's in their work, in their health, in relationships, in their knowledge-gaining or in their self-improvement. A great many men consciously or subconsciously make these decisions on a daily basis. They mostly live their lives in a mediocre fashion because that's 'easier'. But they could take just one area and commit to it 100% (Not 110% - nobody can do that. Where are they going to get the other 10% from? From me? From you?). They could allow themselves to be the best they could possibly be in that area. I repeat, the best they could possibly be. Note that I'm saying 'be' and not 'do', because finding the purest form of you is very much about being. It's also about your attitude rather than the quality of what you produce. It's about allowing yourself to fill your being to the absolute maximum. A god embraces Full-fill-ment

If you were to take away all your excuses, all your bad habits, all your delaying tactics, all your running away and deflection, what would happen? What would that feel like? Probably pretty scary for most people. But you could decide to do this in just one area at first. For example, in your health. You could make the decision right now that, without being fanatical, you're going to care for yourself. Would that work for you? I bet it would. And I bet that if you were totally caring for yourself it would have positive impacts on all the other aspects of your life: your general wellbeing, your work, your relationships, your outside interests. Everything. When you feel better in your health and you feel better about yourself, you will feel better about everyone and everything in your life. You will also be able to inhabit the purest form of you and your Higher Self.

Actor or audience

In life you can choose to be either an actor or a member of the audience watching the action. If you're happy about just being a member of that audience then that's your prerogative. But that's one of the aspects that distinguishes a god from other men. If you want to be a god then you have to be that actor. And by acting I don't mean pretending. I mean taking action: fully engaging with life. You will have to examine your life and study it in detail. Then, once you've studied it, you will need to address all the areas that you can perfect.

As I said earlier, behind all of your behaviour and everything that you do in life you will give yourself permission to act. Every moment of the day you are making subconscious decisions and giving yourself permission to act on those decisions. These decisions range from the almost infinitesimal to the critical. If we were totally aware we would notice that there is a gateway through which we can either allow passage or deny it. Think about it. What are you doing right now? Standing, sitting, lying, leaning? Why did you choose to be this way? Somewhere along the way you made that choice. You could have made another, different, decision.

So, to repeat: you can actually choose to be a god. You can decide that right now without any prevarication. You can give yourself permission. You can also choose to do and be all the things that it takes to fully embody that god. It's your choice, your decision. Or you could decide to do and be only some of these things. Again, that's your prerogative.

3: THE QUALITIES THAT A GOD POSSESSES

> **'The most natural way of behaving is with integrity. There is no other way'**

Here, in no particular order, are some qualities which you can develop in order to enrich your god-ness.

Dignity

A god behaves with dignity at all times. He takes the higher path and rises above petty arguments, Whether or not you behave with dignity speaks volumes about you. It also demonstrates to others how you feel about yourself.

That's not to say you probably won't let your emotions get the better of you sometimes. (This is, after all, about being a god, not a robot.) But, even at your most emotional, it is important to be clear about not blaming others. For example, if you're feeling angry, remember that it's your anger. Another person is simply a trigger for that anger. Nobody can make you angry. It's your reaction to the trigger which brings about the anger. Ultimately you have the choice whether to react to that trigger with anger or not. If you do choose that path (or if you're behaving unconsciously) it's especially important not to dump your anger on innocent parties. It's certainly acceptable to express any anger that you feel. In fact it's important, because you certainly don't want that energy trapped inside you. But the way you express that anger is important. Yell, scream, punch a cushion or a punching-bag. But do that by yourself. And if someone has done or said something which triggers your anger, then tell them that. With *dignity*. And while acknowledging that it's *your* anger and not trying to make them take the 'blame'.

Dignity means respecting yourself, but also respecting others. In fact it means respecting *all* living beings. Respecting not only their right to exist, but honouring them as well. And, as everyone (and everything) is joined – not so much at the hip, but in our collective unconscious – by respecting and honouring others you are also respecting and honouring yourself. And vice versa.

In order to achieve this, the first factor to be considered is your ego. Do you always have to be 'right'? Do you need to have the last word? Is it important that other people believe what you believe or agree with what you say?

If so, why?

If you're having a discussion with others it is simply enough to present your case. If you are challenged by others it is acceptable to answer those challenges in a calm, thoughtful way. However, it is not necessary to keep hammering away at someone until you beat them into submission with your ideas. If they don't agree with you then they don't agree. You may consider them ignorant or uninformed. But that's their problem. Not yours. So don't make it yours.

Likewise, if someone criticizes you it's fair enough to present your case without feeling defensive. If you do feel defensive it would be good to look at why you do. Does it feel like an unjust criticism? Again: their criticism is not your problem (unless, of course, that person is influencing others' decisions involving you). Then, as above, simply state your truth and leave it at that.

It would be more relevant for you to look at the emotions that others' criticism brings up in you. Do you feel misunderstood? Do you feel slighted or traduced? Do you feel hurt? And can you remember when, in your life, you first felt this emotion? Was it when you were a small boy? Oh, yes, that's right. The parts of you that object to the criticism are your ego and the small boy inside you: "It's not fair!" No, it may not be fair. It may be completely unwarranted and even completely wrong. But so what! You know the truth. You have conveyed your truth about the subject to others. Leave it at that.

And I've got news for you: It's None of Your Business! Whatever anyone says about you is up to them. You can't stop them (unless you sue them for defamation). And see this: It's their criticism. And if they choose to believe something about you which is not your truth, then so be it. Too bad. Be dignified about it. Rise above it. You're probably dealing with unaware fools anyway. Don't waste your energy.

Also you don't have to take on somebody else's emotions. If they're angry or feeling negative ("What a horrible day this is"), that's what *they're* experiencing. It doesn't have to be your experience. You can distance yourself from their feelings and decide for yourself what you want to feel.

Dignity is a fundamental quality of gods. Be dignified in all interactions with others.

Love

It's not just that a god loves. A god *is* love. You are the very essence of love. It is from that wellspring of love that you can love. In particular you have love for the being that you are. When you truly love that being, you will be able to fully inhabit the god that you are.

Love is not a doing thing. Love is a being thing: your heart opens and you feel love; you *are* love; love overwhelms you. And, when you experience love, it is *your* love, it's not about the object of your love.

Love is not conditional, and expecting reciprocation of that love can be very detrimental. It would be a mistake to use it as a bargaining chip.

If we can start by truly loving ourselves and then love everything around us, we will become love. That is enough. The fact that we then feel 'loved' by someone else is a bonus and a blessing. But there cannot be expectations or 'deals' to be made. And another person's love for us cannot replace a lack of love we feel for ourselves.

So many people today do not love themselves. In fact there are many people who believe that loving oneself is actually wrong. They think it means one is vain, self-centred, or narcissistic. But I'm not talking about spending hours in front of mirrors or excluding everyone else from your consciousness. I'm not talking about *only* considering yourself. I'm talking about becoming the very essence of love, so that all you see and all you experience is love.

And the way that you start this process is by *accepting* yourself. Accepting that you're a perfectly imperfect human being who sometimes makes mistakes. Yes, gods make mistakes or errors of judgment. Some people even believe that there is no such thing as a 'mistake'. If you are aware, then a mistake simply becomes a learning experience. Hopefully you will not repeat that 'mistake'.

Once you can accept yourself then you can forgive yourself for all the 'unforgivable' things you have done. And you might as well forgive yourself. There are no time machines. You can't go back and change anything. So, let go of those events. Stuff happens, right? If you get to do it differently another time, then great! If not, then tough! But STOP CARRYING THAT BAGGAGE AROUND WITH YOU. It will do you no good, only harm. Let go. Forgive yourself.

Next, accept others. Accept their mistakes, all the injustices that they created. Rise above it all and be true to your real god-ness. A god doesn't bear grudges. A god doesn't carry that baggage either. Let go of it all and be free. I'm not saying you have to forgive anyone (although that would be good). Or that you have to forget it. I'm saying *accept* it. Whatever it was, it will not do you any good dragging that energy around with you. And, once you can free yourself of that energy you can create a space for love. Take the example of someone who stole money from you. If the money is now unrecoverable and the thief is untouchable I am not suggesting that you simply forgive the thief. Nor am I even proposing that you forget the incident – especially if it helps you to not repeat it. What I am saying is that if you continue to invest your emotions in the incident all that you will be doing will be to harm yourself. Accept that it happened, learn from it, even warn others. But then move on with your life. It is a fact that it happened. You wouldn't have chosen it. But you cannot change history. And now, hanging onto it will only affect you. Nelson Mandela is quoted as having said: "Resentment is like drinking poison and then hoping it will kill your enemies." Focus on other aspects of your life.

But, actually, it goes beyond 'forgiveness' of self or the other. Because what does 'forgiveness' mean to you? For many people it implies that there is 'something' to forgive. In other words, someone has done something 'wrong' which requires forgiveness. It's much more important to think in terms of compassion. If you truly have compassion this will bring about acceptance.

The word 'love' is somewhat overused today. We use it in many contexts. We say that we love someone, or we love our pet, or even a house or a picture.

But think about it for a moment. What are we really saying when we say we 'love'? Really, we're stating something about *ourselves*. We're expressing an emotion; that something makes us feel a certain way. But what if it was the other way around? What if it wasn't anyone or anything that caused you to feel love, but that you were simply filled with love? In other words, you're not responding (or reacting) to a stimulus, but generating love within yourself, and that love emanates from you. So that's why I say that it's not just that a god loves. A god *is* love. You are love. And this love forms a major part of your god-ness.

The next step is to see the positives in anything: any person; any situation; any relationship; any experience; or any object. Because, by focusing on the negatives, you prevent yourself from experiencing love. You might even choose to create a list (either written or unwritten) of the positive aspects of anything. For myself, rather than bringing my attention to 'what is wrong' with someone, I would much prefer to focus on what I like about them – or, indeed, what delights me about them.

Are you able to observe the sunlight through the branches of a tree or shimmering off the ocean - or hear a child's giggle or a bird singing - and just let it touch your heart? Because if you can allow your heart to open and simply observe things without judgment or reaction, then I assure you that love will fill your heart and you will *become* love.

Awareness & Consciousness

Two of the most fundamental qualities of a god are awareness and consciousness. They are very similar, but you could say that one feeds the other in that first you become aware. Then, as it goes deeper, whatever you have become aware of enters your consciousness. The trick is for that process to happen much faster and much more frequently. This happens all the time in your life. At first you might see a bigger picture (whether that's with a person and a relationship or with an object). Then a part of that picture will become clearer to you. This might happen over a period of time.

My parents used to have a painting in their living room. I loved that picture. It had many details in it including figures. It was quite complex and it felt like there was a narrative to this picture. I used to gaze at it frequently, and many times I actually saw some new detail that I hadn't noticed before. This detail entered my consciousness and contributed to the story being told by the picture. This happens also in relationships. A person may tell you something or show you a different aspect of themselves which helps you to gain better awareness of who they are and, often, how that impacts on your relationship with them. By opening yourself to becoming aware in this fashion you will achieve greater insight which, in turn, can be applied to that person and, perhaps, future situations.

Awareness covers all aspects of your life. Especially yourself, but also everything and everyone around you.

Awareness about yourself

"The Enlightenment" was a European intellectual movement of the 17th and 18th centuries emphasizing reason and individualism. It was heavily influenced by 17th-century philosophers such as Descartes, Rousseau, Diderot, Voltaire, and Isaac Newton. It really began to gain strength when the English political philosopher John Locke published *Essay Concerning Human Understanding*, in which understanding plays a fundamental role In other words: Before you can develop or change anything, first you have to understand it. And this also applies to you. You must gain as much knowledge and understanding about yourself as possible. Then you will be able to fully realize your true potential.

This is all about getting to know, understand, and accept yourself. It's also about developing and heightening all of your senses. It is essential to be aware of both your mental processes and your emotions.

Start with your behaviour. What affects that? There are many causes, of course. Much of it will be learned behaviour, either taught to you by others or developed by you over the course of your life. Of course, you will also be profoundly affected by your emotions and your thoughts.

Learn to sift through, identify and distinguish your emotions. What are you feeling right now as you read this? Can you identify any emotion(s). A lot of men will say they're not feeling *anything*. But, if they close their eyes and begin to tune in, they discover that there are often either strong current emotions or residual emotions that they're carrying.

And, if all you can think of in terms of emotions, are 'happy', 'sad' and 'angry', it may also be time to update your emotional vocabulary:

In order to help you, here is a partial list of possible emotions:
Abandoned, accepted, afraid, affectionate, aggravated, alarmed, amiable, angry, annoyed, anxious, awkward, baffled, bashful, bewildered, bitter, blue, bored, bothered, brave, calm, caring, cautious, changeable, cheery, clever, clumsy, comical, compassionate, competent, confident, confused, considerate, content, contrary, cooperative, cranky, curious, daring, defiant, delighted, depressed, destructive, detached, determined, devastated, devious, disappointed, discouraged, disempowered, disgusted, disillusioned, disorganized, dumb, eager, edgy, embarrassed, empathetic, encouraged, energetic, enthusiastic, envious, excited, exhausted, expectant, exuberant, fearful, flustered, foolish, forgiving, fortunate, friendly, frustrated, furious, generous, grateful, great, greedy, grief-stricken, grouchy, grumpy, guilty, gullible, happy, haughty, heartbroken, helpless, hesitant, honest, hopeless, horrified, hum-

ble, humiliated, hurt, ignorant, ignored, impatient, impotent, inadequate, indifferent, insecure, inspired, interested, invisible, irked, irrational, irritated, irresponsible, jaded, jealous, joyful, judgmental, jumpy, keen, lacklustre, lazy, leery, lonely, lost, loving, lucky, mad, magical, malevolent, manipulated, manipulative, maternal, mean, meek, mellow, melodramatic, mischievous, miserable, mistrustful, misunderstood, mixed-up, modest, moody, mopey, naive, nasty, naughty, nauseated, nerdy, nervous, noble, neglected, neglectful, needy, needed, nonchalant, nonplussed, obedient, odd, obliging, obsessive, obstinate, offended, out-of-control, outraged, overjoyed, overloaded, overpowered, overstimulated, panicked, patronized, peaceful, peeved, pensive, petty, petulant, picky, playful, pleased, powerful, powerless, preoccupied, proud, psyched, puzzled, quarrelsome, questioning, quiet, rageful, rational, rattled, reactive, reasonable, reassured, rebellious, refreshed, relaxed, relieved, reluctant, remorseful, repulsed, resentful, reserved, respected, restful, restive, sad, safe, satisfied, scared, scornful, secure, sensitive, serene, serious, shy, silly, smiley, smug, snarky, snarly, sociable, sorry, spiteful, stressed-out, stubborn, stupid, surprised, talkative, tearful, temperamental, terrific, terrified, thoughtful, threatened, timid, tired, tolerant, torn, touched, trusted, trusting, trustworthy, ugly, unafraid, unappreciated, uncomfortable, uneasy, uncertain, understanding, understood, unimpressed, unruffled, useless, uneasy, undecided, unique, unruly, unsafe, up, vacant, vain, valued, vibrant, victorious, violent, vital, vivacious, vexed, volatile, vulnerable, wacky, warm, wary, weak, weary, weepy, weird, whimsical, whiny, wilful, wishful, wistful, withdrawn, witty, woeful, worn out, worried, worthless, wound up, wronged, yearning, yielding, youthful, yucky, zany, zapped, zealous, zen, zestful, zippy,

Phew! Quite a list, isn't it? At any time of the day you are probably feeling at least one — and possibly several — of these feelings. And there are many emotions which are not on this list.

So, I ask you again: What are you feeling right now as you read this? Take your time and feel. You don't need to let these emotions control your life, but it's important to know and appreciate what you are currently feeling.

Identifying your emotion(s) is the first part of this equation. The second part is to understand why you are feeling any particular emotion. This requires greater focus. Some emotions appear to be simple. But, in fact, they're often not so straightforward as they appear. For example: you're driving along in your car, feeling okay with the world. Suddenly, and seemingly for no apparent reason, another car passes you and pulls in directly in front of you. It feels as though the driver of this vehicle cut you off and you become angry. Why? What just happened that brought about this emotion? For each of us it might be different. But, for many, it feels personal, as though the other driver personally challenged you. This goes directly to the male ego, and you might have what is probably a very ancient reaction that goes back to prehistoric times. It's likely that, in order to protect you from harm, sudden extra shots of adrenalin and testosterone were released into your system. You might also have a feeling of someone invading your space, something we feel very protective about. There might also be a subconscious feeling of fear. And we don't like to be made fearful, so you might feel especially resentful towards the other driver. In addition, some of the anger that you experienced was probably related to other events in your life, perhaps events that happened when you were a small boy.

The point is that there are many reasons to become angry. And *none of them are necessary* in this situation. If your energy was totally aligned when an incident like this happened you might have been able to allow the adrenalin to increase, breathe through the whole experience and simply take it as just another small incident. Especially not as something to be taken personally. Most probably that driver doesn't even know who you are.

To be clear: I'm not saying that anger *per se* is a bad thing. I'm pointing out that there are many reasons for it which you could identify so that you can know yourself better and become more aware.

By the way, I believe that, if you're feeling anger, then you should at least acknowledge it to yourself. Pretending not to feel anger is about *less* awareness, not more.

And anger is considered to be a simple emotion. What about a more complex emotion such as feeling uneasy. Are you able to analyse what's going on with you? Where is the lack of ease coming from? Is it physical, emotional or psychological (or a combination)? Is it from a verbal exchange that you had? Does it have to do with your expectations in some way? Is there fear there (and, if so, where's that coming from)? Do you feel threatened in some way? Do you feel 'out of place'? Are you uncomfortable in the company of the people you are currently with (and, again, if so why)? Or is it something more esoteric? Is it to do with the feng shui of the room where you are? Are you able to tune into the specific reason(s) why you feel uneasy?

Again, it's not about being critical of your emotions. It's about awareness. And it's also about understanding. Because, with understanding comes acceptance. And, when you can accept everything about yourself, you can accept that you are in fact a god.

Once you can be aware of your emotions you can also begin to see how you react *from* those emotions. And let me be very clear here: I'm not talking about responding. Responding is a natural occurrence. On the other hand, what we frequently do is to react from an unconscious place. A place which quite possibly has nothing whatsoever to do with what's happening in your life right now. Try it for yourself. Somebody does something or says something and you react to that. Why are you reacting? And exactly what are you really reacting to? What is at the heart of your reaction? Is your ego involved in some way? Does it remind you of a previous time when you felt hurt (or another emotion) – or even something that's happening in your life at the moment, but which has nothing to do with this action? If you are simply reacting, then that is an *un*conscious response. So be aware and be clear with what's happening. See whether your response is actually a kneejerk reaction. If it is then reconsider this response. Be aware and take responsibility for your actions.

There are so many emotions that we have which are directly linked to our subconscious, and we're often barely aware of the connection. All we seem to know is that we're feeling them. But there are a few emotions which seemingly have stronger connections to our consciousness over which we might have better management. An example of these is guilt, which I will go into more deeply later on.

Developing awareness in other areas

It is necessary to develop *all* of your senses. We have five dominant senses and something we refer to as our 'sixth sense'. (I actually believe that we have a great deal more senses, and that we could develop our ability to tune into those other senses. But that's a subject for another book.)

The five dominant senses, credited to Aristotle, are sight, hearing, touch, smell, and taste. And you can develop all of these. Here are some simple exercises that you can do:

Sight

There are several exercises for you to develop your sight

An old party game is for someone to place a number of objects (say 20) on a tray and then cover them all with a cloth. When that person uncovers the objects you have a short period of time to see and remember them. They are re-covered and then it is your turn to name each of the objects. This game not only trains your memory, it teaches you to *see* things.

In advanced driving courses a driver will notice and describe out loud other vehicles, individuals and all of their actions on the road as they're driving along. For example, "The white car in front of me is slowing down. In between us there is a bicycle going slowly and wobbling slightly. The van behind me is very close to my rear. The oncoming traffic has slowed to a crawl. Further ahead I can see a pedestrian deciding whether or not to cross the road." You can do this as you drive along and it will definitely develop your sight awareness.

Another little exercise is to find a leaf. Take the time to really look at it. How big is it? What shape is it? Is it rounded, pointy, spiky? What shade of what colour is it? Does it have veins or ribs, and how many are there? Does it have small hairs growing outwards from it? What else can you observe about it?

You can also take the time to take notice of – and delight in – the small things around you. Focus on one object, describe it to yourself, then move on to the next. Do it as slowly as you can.

Your general awareness should be the same way that you walk along the street. It is important to be aware of what is around you. If you only see what is in front of you, you might trip or fall in a hole. If you only look down, you will miss everything else in your life.

Hearing

Make yourself comfortable somewhere. Close your eyes. Begin to tune into the different sounds around you. What can you hear? You'll probably first hear those sounds closest to you. There might be someone talking. There might be music, the sound of machinery, a baby crying, a clock ticking, animal noises, vehicles driving by. Then extend your range. What can you hear further away?

Separate each of those sounds. Try and count how many individual sounds you can hear.

Even if it's really quiet you will be able to hear something. It might just be your own breathing or the air against your ear, or even the sound of your pulse inside your head. Learn to become aware of not only these sounds, but other, unusual sounds that you're not used to hearing.

After you've done this for a while open your eyes. Try and still hear all those sounds and distinguish between them.

If you do this on a regular basis your awareness of individual sounds will increase. And, together with all your other senses, your overall awareness will develop.

Touch

One excellent way to develop your touch awareness is massage – both giving and receiving. And I'm talking about very gentle massage. If you have a partner this can have additional benefits.

When giving a massage, allow first the tips of your fingers, then the rest of your hands to explore the body you're touching. Feel the warmth of the skin, feel the smoothness or otherwise of that skin's surface. Explore the curves of the body and the way that the various parts of the body join together. Discover soft flesh and harder, bonier parts. Feel the response of that body to your touch. Put all of your awareness into your hands, especially your finger tips (it might help to close your eyes) and take it all in.

Hopefully your partner will really enjoy the experience, but do this initially as an awareness exercise. If it later develops into something else, well.....all the better.

When receiving a massage feel where the masseur's hands are going. Breathe deeply and bring your attention to each of your body parts in turn as they're touched. Make your skin a receptor – a canvas for the masseur's hands to paint on.

You can also sensitize your finger tips to various surfaces, from extremely rough to very smooth, from sandpaper or the bristles of a brush, for example, to the finest of fine silk.

Taste

How developed is your sense of taste. If someone presented you with a dish without telling you what was in it, could you identify the main ingredients? Can you distinguish between different types of foodstuffs. For example, if you eat meat could you categorically say whether something is beef or lamb? If you weren't told, would you know whether you were eating chicken or fish in a sandwich? Can you identify what herbs are in a dish? (And how familiar are you, in any case, with different herbs and spices.) Without looking, would you know whether you were drinking red wine or white?

Another great party game is to blindfold a taster. Present them with something on a spoon and get them to identify what it is. You can ask a friend, partner or family member to do the same for you. Have them prepare a range of things (they don't have to be normal food, but obviously, you don't want to be poisoned). Then get them to present them to you one by one. Once you've been able to do this successfully they might start to refine the process. They can even ask you to distinguish between different types of cheese. (If you're a vegan, sorry. In that case you might like to say whether they are presenting you with cabbage or cauliflower for example – often this is not as easy as it sounds.)

Smell

Of the five dominant senses, the sense of smell is possibly the hardest to develop. But it can be refined. However, firstly, you need to ascertain what your current abilities are. Do you suffer from hay fever or a blocked nose? And if you smoke you're probably only able to smell a fraction of available aromas.

Unless we come across a pungent odor, we're often unaware of the various smells in our lives. Certainly, if there's a sudden pong, or someone walks into the room wearing a strong perfume, or coffee is brewing or food is cooking, then we notice it. But, often it's more subtle than that. For example, you might become hungry for no apparent reason. Then, after a while, you realize that you can smell onions cooking. But that can take a while. However, you can learn to become aware of smells much earlier.

Of course you might ask why you would want to become aware of smells. The answer is because it helps in developing your levels of awareness generally (what this whole section is all about).

And, don't forget, your sense of smell affects how much you enjoy the taste of food and, therefore, your general enjoyment of life. And also, in case you've forgotten why you're developing all of your senses, it's so that that you can be the best possible *you* that you can be and to get the most out of life.

The Sixth sense

Call it intuition. Call it psychic powers. Call it whatever you like, a great many people have discovered for themselves that they have a sixth sense. And you can too. The first step in developing this sense is to acknowledge that you have a sixth sense, so that you can make yourself available to it. And, in order to access this sense, you will need to be able to relax completely at will, even while standing or moving, and eventually even in a crowded room. Of course this requires practice and patience. But it is integral in becoming totally aware.

You will have to decide whether what you're feeling is simply a conscious thought, an emotion, or an actual sense of something else. If there's a conscious thought or an emotion, then you have to divorce yourself from that enough to tune in.

Learn to trust your intuition. As above, if you feel uncomfortable in a room, for example, ask yourself why. Look at what's going on inside you. Is it that you feel uncomfortable standing for a long period of time or that you gain nothing from being with the group of people in the room? Do you find the décor unpleasant to be around? Or is there something else going on? If you can find no logical reason as to why you feel uncomfortable then the chances are that your sixth sense is sending you a message.

To begin developing your intuition you can start by paying attention to any additional message or information that comes to you, not from something that you might have been told, but from elsewhere Be open to this 'knowing' without judging it. Trust the experience, whether you believe in a sixth sense or not. You might even like to make notes of any of these experiences and review them at a later date.

Similarly, try to remember any dreams that you have. Keep a pen and paper by your bed to make notes as soon as you wake up. Try not to interpret the dream at the time, just make careful notes. Also record the emotion(s) that came with the dream. Later you can look at the dream and feel any significance for yourself. You can perform the same process if you meditate.

There is also a useful exercise that you can carry out last thing at night: Go through your day from start to finish. Remember what you did, who you were with, what emotion you were feeling. (I also like to be thankful for all of the experiences that I had during the day, especially the 'good' ones.) Some people actually like to keep 'gratitude diaries'. Many people like to remember their friends and family at this time, taking the time to dwell for a moment on each one.

You will also find that the more you develop your dominant senses, the more your sixth sense will also develop.

Another very important sense

Before we leave senses altogether, there's another 'sense' that is vital to develop: A sense of humour. I'm not talking about telling jokes or laughing at people falling over on Youtube (although the ability to just relax and laugh is important). I'm talking about the ability to laugh in the face of adversity.

Everybody has challenges in life, big and small, often on a daily basis. If you can see them for what they are, 'challenges', you might be able to change your perception. I'm not suggesting that if you were diagnosed with a fatal disease that you should simply laugh about it. I'm proposing that, after the initial shock, part of your process might be to see all aspects of the situation.

And so it is with lesser challenges. For example: you're running late for an appointment, the traffic is terrible and you feel like tearing your hair out or screaming. It's easy to get caught up in small things and it's necessary to gain some perspective. If you can think laterally in this situation, you might be able to not only reduce your stress levels (and possibly live longer), but you will be stronger in yourself, more integrated and more easily inhabit your god-ness.

What do I mean by think laterally? In the above case, for example, you could take yourself out of the picture subjectively and see yourself simply as a character in a comedy movie where everything is going wrong. In other words, see the lighter side of events. Yes, you might feel that the outcome of this appointment is very important. But, if you've done everything you can do to let other people know, then you might as well relax, breathe deeply and trust that whatever happens will be the right outcome. It's not that nothing matters, it's that you can take a different approach to your life and who you are.

Integrity

As a realized god your energy is clear and uncluttered. You are one with yourself and the universe. Therefore the most natural way of behaving is with integrity. There is no other way.

Take responsibility for your actions and your communication. If you say that you're going to do something, then do your utmost to do it. Remember, this is not about keeping your promises to other people and worrying about letting them down, it's about *your* integrity. This is how a god behaves. At the end of the day, however, if you find that you really can't do what you said you were going to do, then tell others clearly and as soon as possible. Do not concern yourself with the emotion of 'letting someone down' or even letting yourself down. Be practical and pragmatic and move on.

Part of your integrity is in your communication with others. Be clear in your speech. Speak your truth from your heart with authenticity. Be direct without concerning yourself with possible consequences. Because, if you are speaking your truth from your heart with authenticity, then somebody else's reaction is not your problem. If they can't understand your truth then, by all means, rephrase your message. But, remember, if you've spoken with authenticity and as clearly as possible, it's not your duty to *make* them understand. If they can't comprehend what you're saying – or if they disagree with you – then the onus is on them.

This becomes especially true if you're making a request. A major part of this is about your self-esteem. If you're asking for something, do you totally believe that you deserve it? Do you feel that another person might refuse you? Is fear present in you? Look at those questions and answer them. Then ask for what you want without recourse to intimidation, manipulation, circumlocution or self-deprecation,

Mean what you say, and say what you mean. Communicate clearly and frequently. Be transparent in that communication. If you ask for anything don't be obscure or talk about things in a roundabout way. Don't hint or make unnecessary references. And, most importantly don't imply anything, assuming that the person you're talking to will automatically know what you're talking about.

What is it that you'd really like to say? Say *that*.

Here are a few other ways to build your integrity:

- Be reliable. Show up on time, every time. (As above) if you make an agreement always do your utmost to complete that agreement. If you see that, in spite of your best attempts, you're going to have to break the agreement, communicate that clearly and as early as possible. Keep your promises.
- It is important that you are straight and sincere when you deal with people. Don't pretend to agree with someone if you disagree. You can remain neutral if you choose, rather than having to give your perspective. But don't be fake.
- If you make a mistake admit that mistake to yourself and others. Remember you can use mistakes as an opportunity for improvement.
- Be honest in all your dealings with others. Never cheat, lie, or try to manipulate others to give yourself an unfair advantage. Over the years I have had people say to me something like: "My being involved in your business will bring in other customers/will lend prestige to your business, therefore you should give me a financial discount." This is generally untrue and is just a cheap bargaining technique. It is dishonest and certainly lacks integrity.

One other thing: be clear inside yourself what are your ethics and values right now, and be true to those. I would define morality as something which is decided by society and imposed on the individual, so I'm not talking about morality. I'm talking about what is right for *you*. Of course ethics and values often vary during our lifetimes – especially as we mature. However, it's important that you maintain your integrity by being aligned with your own ethics and values as they stand now.

Authenticity

The existentialist philosopher Søren Kierkegaard proposed that each individual, rather than society or religion, is solely responsible for giving meaning to his life and living it passionately and sincerely (that is: 'authentically'). It is your responsibility as a god to be 100% authentic, without hiding behind *any* kind of mask.

How do other people see you? What face do you present to the world? Are you conscious of presenting yourself in a particular way – a way which is not who you 'really are' in your heart of hearts. If so, why are you doing this? Is it so that others will like you or love you or respect you more? Is it so that you'll get on better in your job or your social circle? Do you, in fact, have a secret fear that you're going to get found out, that someday others will discover that you're not who you've been pretending to be? Many, many men do this. They often have a mask or a persona which they present to the world, but which is not *them*, and they are not being true to who they really are. They are not being authentic. And, since authenticity is one of the highest principles of being a god, they can never truly their god-ness.

There are some men who just find it difficult to show the world who they really are. It makes them feel too vulnerable. And that is painful and scary for them. Some of these men develop personas and become 'characters'. Then they hide behind those personas. Many of these men appear to be extroverts, wearing outlandish clothes and wearing their hair or beards flamboyantly. But they're often actors, playing a version of themselves, and all this is to distract you from seeing who they really are. And, of course, often they're afraid that what they are is 'nothing'. Or worse: someone who is 'detestable'.

Now, I'm not criticizing these men. They're entitled to behave any way they choose, and some of them are simply irrepressible extroverts who love dressing up. However, in many instances they're often a good example of not being authentic. If you are extrovert by nature or you frequently find yourself in this situation, just be clear in yourself why you are like this. Are you just expressing your joy with the world and being creative with yourself, or are you hiding?

Think about it. If you create and present a persona, then you are not being honest. Your energy is not flowing as it should, and you will not be able to fulfil your highest state. On some level you will always be conscious of it and there will always be – however small – some discomfort.

Far better to be true to yourself. Always speak *your* truth (even the smaller truths). And, I can't say this often enough: think your own thoughts; speak your own thoughts, not somebody else's (especially the truisms and platitudes that you read on social media); listen to others, but make up your own mind; and be yourself – the god that you are.

Of course it's important to discover and know who you are, what you want in life, and what your values are. It is also essential to hold your own beliefs – not somebody else's, whether that's your family, teachers, community, friends – or even me. (Start right away: are those last sentences true for you?).

Begin with thinking about your priorities. What do you want in life? What is important to you? What kind of lifestyle do you want? What makes you happy? What kind of relationship(s) do you want? Write down answers to all of these questions as they come to you, in no particular order. Then go through the list and really think about how important each answer is to you. When you've done that, start to number the answers with the most important (to you) at the top, and the least important at the bottom.

THE GOD THAT YOU ARE

Of course, throughout your life, many of these answers will change. But these are your values right now.

Once you have your own values you will start to get a sense of who *you* are, rather than parroting somebody else's words, actions or values. Now it is time to be strong and be true to your values. This doesn't mean that you never listen to anybody else. On the contrary, a god always has an open mind. He will listen to others respectfully, without filtering the content through his ego or entrenched beliefs. Then he will examine the information to see whether all or some of it resonates with him. If it does he will be prepared to accept it. Otherwise he will disregard what doesn't resonate.

A god will also behave authentically rather than following the herd. "Is this action true for me, or am I giving in to peer pressure?" Again: does the action or behaviour resonate with your truth?

A god observes. He does not get caught up in pettiness or somebody else's 'stuff'. You don't have to match an emotion being expressed by another person. If they're angry or discouraged or agitated or being obstinate, you don't have to follow suit. Take responsibility for your own actions and emotions and let them take responsibility for theirs. If you feel antagonism from somebody else, that's not *your* antagonism, it's theirs. And if you feel love from another that's not *your* love, it's theirs. So what are you *really* feeling? Is it a response (or a reaction) or is it an authentic emotion. Be authentic. You are not a robot

There are occasions in life where you have agreements. Some of these are verbal or even written, and some of them are tacit. They might, for example, include your relationships (including with your children) or your employment. In these cases you most definitely have certain obligations which you should always do your best to honour.

But, outside of these occasions, remember that you don't owe anyone anything. You certainly don't owe them any explanations, whether that's for your life choices, decisions, priorities or beliefs…..or anything else. And you don't have to say 'yes' to everything that everyone asks of you. Your obligation is to yourself. If it doesn't feel right don't say 'yes'. This is not being 'selfish', it's just being realistic with your priorities. If you are the sort of man who always says 'yes' you might want to look at why you do that. Is there fear there if you say 'no'? (I'm not suggesting that you should always say 'no', I'm saying that you should balance what's asked of you against, what you realistically can – and want – to do.) And, if you are the sort of man who always says 'yes', saying 'no' occasionally can be very liberating.

In fact, one area that you could look at is how susceptible you are to others trying to impose guilt trips on you or attempting to emotionally blackmail you. Beware especially of others endeavouring to make you feel guilty about something that you've done or haven't done so that they can manipulate your feelings, and therefore manipulate you. If you feel this to be the case there is no need to overreact. Just be clear with that person about your right to behave in a way that suits you. At this time a manipulative person might actually react themselves and tell you that you're selfish. Be aware that this is just another attempt to control you.

How you choose to live life is your business and nobody else's. it's not your responsibility to explain or justify anything about yourself to anybody. If they don't like something about you or the way you do things, that's *their* problem, not yours. Neither do you have to try to impress anybody. And your religious and political views are not anybody else's business either. You don't have to convince them of your views (as though you're so unsure of these views that your ego requires others to be on your 'side' in order to validate you). What you believe is what you believe. And neither do you need to defend your views. Having an exchange of ideas is healthy, but that's all.

One area to look at is whether you behave differently towards people with whom you have a relationship rather than strangers. Are you more inclined to acquiesce to the former? Why? Is it out of love, or are you fearful of damaging those relationships? And are you then being authentic in those relationships. One of the major themes in this book is about your boundaries and being true to yourself. If you acquiesce unthinkingly you might want to look at what's really going on for you. Are you being true to the god that you are?

Who is the authentic you?

These are questions which few men ask themselves: "Who am I?" "Who is the authentic me?". As men, we are inclined to take on 'roles'. We are sons, brothers, fathers. We identify with our skills and our employment, our teams, our cultures. But who are you? What is it that makes you a unique human being? What is your essence, the essential you? Is there something unchanging in you that you were born with and you will die with? Are there parts of you that will develop as you get older? What is the authentic you?

Of course these questions are lifelong questions. And, sometimes we never find the answers. But it is essential that you do your best to try and answer them. Because, until you find the authentic you, it will be difficult to know precisely where to establish your boundaries.

You can say that you have certain needs and wants. You can defend your territory, not letting someone else step over the line. But boundaries are about so much more than this. They're also about opinions and beliefs. When you speak, whose beliefs do you profess? Whose voice are you using? Are you just repeating something that has been fed to you from friends, politicians, the mass media, your parents, your religious leaders or something you read on social media?

Stop for a moment. Have you really thought about this subject? Have you truly thought through both sides of the argument. Have you discussed it with others and *listened to them*? Have you conducted some research into it? Or are you just *agreeing* with somebody else? Because that's not being authentic. As I said earlier, it's not necessary to have an opinion about everything. But, when you do express an opinion, just be clear that it's *your* opinion. This applies whether we're talking about some of the weightier subjects like euthanasia, capital punishment, abortion, same-sex marriage, or refugees. It also applies to areas like sex and drugs. Where do *you* stand? And, even if you're simply discussing music and arts, don't simply follow the rest of the herd, be true to yourself.

It's also important to never lie to yourself. Even if you find yourself pretending to others (lying by omission *or* commission), at the very least own your truth to yourself. Be clear inside yourself what is real and what is not real. Because a god owes that to himself.

How well do you know yourself? Can you be truly honest with yourself? If so, are you aware when you're being 'real' and when you're not? And, more to the point, are you aware when you're being fake or just shallow? Of course, to an extent, being 'real' is highly subjective. There's often a cultural template that overlays and rules all 'acceptable' behaviour. So, for example, in some cultures it's necessary for men to behave in a macho way. These men are pure bravado. Other ways of describing that way of being are arrogance, bluster, or braggadocio. In other words, these are acts that are assumed; they are behaviours that do not reflect how the man is actually feeling, but how he is pretending to feel. He may, in fact, not be being *who* he is, and is therefore not being *true* to who he is. He is probably doing this to prove something to other people, and, in many cases, he is overcompensating for feelings of inferiority. Because, if he was comfortable in himself, he wouldn't need to pretend to be something that he isn't.

This is also often coupled with the fact that many men are not comfortable with their emotions. Either they've been brought up to believe that a true 'man' doesn't feel (let alone show) his emotions, or he actually becomes overwhelmed by his emotions. He might have the subconscious belief that if he were to allow himself to feel his emotions he might fall apart. And, of course, he must never allow this to happen! So he puts on an act.

Do you find yourself doing this? Do you need to pretend to be something that you're not in order to feel comfortable? If so, you might like to ask yourself why you do this. And, likewise, you might like to consider that you're not being true to yourself – being authentic – when you do it.

On the other hand, you might feel that if others really knew you, that they wouldn't like you. So you keep your emotional life hidden from others. But whatever you hide from others, you are also likely to hide from yourself. And whatever you hide from yourself can control you without your being aware of it.

Learn to check in with your emotions from time to time. What emotion(s) are you experiencing? Do you acknowledge that emotion? You don't have to understand it or even accept it right now. You can work on that later. But – again – be honest with yourself, and at least acknowledge it.

Authenticity comes also with knowing yourself better; what motivates you, what drives you. Once you start to see, for example, "Oh, I'm reacting to this situation because of something that happened to me in the past". You can not only get in touch with who you are, you can actually modify your responses.

Being authentic is also about how you interact with others. Many of us are actually taught as children to put on those masks. To pretend to be and behave in different ways to how we actually are. For example, many boys were told not to cry and to 'toughen up'. Even today I hear advice to men to 'man-up', which basically means not to feel your emotions and certainly not to ever show your feelings. It seems that many people are afraid and even ashamed of being vulnerable. They equate vulnerability with weakness. In fact it's completely the other way around. A god acknowledges his vulnerability and THAT MAKES HIM STRONGER. A god knows that he doesn't have to wear a mask; to pretend to others something that is not true. By feeling and expressing all of his emotions not only is a god being authentic and true to himself, he is also growing into a fully-rounded human being, rather than a mannequin in a shop window.

So let others see your true face. Sometimes that might be very difficult. Sometimes it might be painful. You might have to confront a number of fears to do that. But I promise you that, ultimately, it will be worth it. You are, unquestionably, a unique being. Unfortunately many of us often seem to see that in a negative light. That we stand out from the crowd (in a 'bad' way), that we will not be accepted. At the bottom of this is a deep, prehistorically-related fear that comes from the time when we lived in groups in caves. In those times if we weren't 'accepted' by the group then we might be thrown out of the cave, and therefore probably would die. So the fear of not being accepted is directly related to the fear of dying. But that isn't the case today. If you think that you're not going to be accepted there is no need to feel as though you're going to die. So what if others don't accept you! That's their problem not yours. Your job is to be acceptable to *yourself*. And that means not pretending. It means being true to the essence of who you *really* are.

The irony of all of that is that when you actually do accept yourself, when you can behave in — and relate from — your authentic self, then you will feel confident. And people are attracted to strong, confident people. Women, in particular, are attracted to confident men.

Are you a pleaser? Do you often find yourself in the position of feeling like you're trying to resolve relationship problems (even ones that don't involve you)? Are you frequently trying to satisfy others? Do you sometimes feel as though you're 'walking on eggshells' so that you don't antagonise others? Well, stop doing those things! You are not actually doing yourself any favours by doing them. And, ultimately, you're not doing others any favours either — let them live their own lives.

If you repeatedly find yourself alone, trying to resolve relationship problems, and others don't seem to be coming to the party, then it's time to ask yourself why. Why does it feel like it's just you? Is it because others are not interested in putting in as much energy as you? In which case, simply state your case. Tell them about your feelings and your thoughts, and inform them that you will wait for a nominated time period to respond. If they don't respond, then it's almost certainly time to move on, whether we're talking about intimate relationships, friendships or business relationships. (Family relationships are a little trickier, but the principle is the same.)

If you regularly feel as though you're trying to satisfy others, consider these possibilities: Many men feel inadequate in themselves; they feel as though they are not 'enough'. They constantly have to do things or say things, be a certain way, to please others. Well, when you realize that you are a god, you will also realize that it's not up to you to please or satisfy others. It's actually NOT up to you to satisfy *anyone*. It's up to *them* to feel satisfied.

And it seems that, for one reason or another, there are many people in the world whom you cannot satisfy. There's a hole in them that can't be filled. NOT EVEN BY YOU.

So, be true to yourself. If it's your goddess, love her with all your heart. By all means speak those words of love, give her gifts, and do things for her, but do all these because you love her, not because you're trying to please or satisfy her.

And, if you ever feel as though you're 'walking on eggshells', then I have to tell you that you are allowing yourself to be manipulated (not necessarily by others, possibly by your own negative thoughts). You are not being true to yourself; you are not being authentic; and your god-ness has gone for a walk!

Be real. In other words be who you *really* are – not who you think other people want you to be. And accept and celebrate your uniqueness. There's nobody else the same as you, and that's wonderful. It is your gift to humanity. That very essence of who you are is the very essence of your god-ness.

Honour

Behave honourably and honestly in all things. A god doesn't need to cheat; a god doesn't need to lie, a god doesn't need to deceive, and a god definitely doesn't need to steal. You are not a beggar, you're a god. The feeling that you might need to resort to any of the above is driven by your fears and a god is aware of his fears, even if he can't conquer them all.

When we use that word 'lie' we mostly think about telling untruths and, of course, it is often tempting to do that. But, as I said, a god doesn't need to do that. However, there is another type of lie: when, you tell a lie by omission rather than by commission. For example, when you're having a conversation with your beloved and you 'conveniently' leave out information that you don't want her to know. This is often just as big a lie as if you told her an untruth.

Why would you do that? Do you genuinely want to deceive your beloved about some aspect of you or your life? Do you want to pretend that you're something which you're not?

Are you being altruistic and trying to protect your beloved from something which you think might hurt her? If this is the case, I suggest that you really think this through. And really get to *know* your beloved – in the past has she given you some indication that she'd actually prefer to know the truth, even if she does feel hurt by that. Or has she conveyed that she'd rather not know. My experience has been that a woman often instinctually knows when you're not telling her the truth. She may not be conscious of this knowledge and that's often worse. Because she may become uneasy because she knows something is 'wrong'.

Or are you afraid of repercussions if you do actually talk about what's happening? This fear, whether it's a fear of confrontation or fear of consequences, can eat away at the heart of a relationship. On a practical level, once either of you closes up to the other in some way the relationship becomes no longer a whole-hearted connection between a god and a goddess, and will also begin to develop fault lines which could form a rift from which it's difficult to recover.

Compassion

A god quite naturally feels compassion. He understands and cares about others. When he witnesses disaster survivors, or people in straitened circumstances or other types of suffering he is moved by the experience and he is sympathetic to those people. When he witnesses suffering in animals he is also moved. But it doesn't have to be major events and circumstances which bring about compassion. In fact, compassion is a natural state in which to exist. And it essentially comes about through empathy, which is both innate and developed. If you can see the plight of others and, without judgment, imagine yourself in their shoes, empathy and compassion will follow. With regard to others' behaviour, one of the best ways that you can develop your empathy is by understanding other people. If you can understand what motivates their behaviour, you will be well along the path to having compassion for them.

And, while we're at it, don't forget to have compassion for yourself as well. In just the same way: if you can understand what motivates you, without having any judgment about it, you will find it easier to be compassionate towards yourself. And this, in turn, will assist you in having more compassion for others.

A god sees behaviour in himself and others which is related to many unconscious and subconscious factors. These are often connected to fears as well as past experiences. A god does not blame – himself or others – he tries to understand. (For more detail on blame please see the chapter "Accept Yourself".) A god has respect for himself and others and also has respect for the planet. And he recognizes all other gods (including animals)

And remember: compassion and love are deeply related. They spring from the same open heart.

Grace

There is a type of feminine grace, an ease of movement that exists. I'm not talking about this. I'm talking about being gracious. I'm talking about how you conduct yourself regardless of gender. I'm talking about being immaculate and elegant in the way that you behave in everything that you do, especially in all your dealings with others. This is also all about acting with finesse and style.

One of the marks of a god is that he recognizes the god in another man and the goddess in a woman. He always treats others with respect and courtesy. If the woman or other man doesn't (or can't) acknowledge this respect and courtesy, then that is not your problem – you will have done what is expected of a god.

This means that sometimes you might have to take 'the high road' and rise above events, whether that's by learning to apologise first or by backing away from an entrenched argument. (Apologising does not make you weak. On the contrary, it is the strong who can apologise with dignity and with grace.) And an entrenched argument is never going to improve the quality of your life. Just think about some of those famous battles in World War I, where a piece of ground was fought over with great loss of life but, in the end, nobody won. So just tuck your ego in and walk away! It will bring you freedom, relief and a better quality of life.

Having grace in your life also means being generous – in all things. That begins with having a generous spirit. And the ways that you can develop a generous spirit are twofold. They are both simple, but require a certain amount of work.

If you really feel your love for humanity you will quite naturally feel generous towards others. Think of a parent's natural love for their child. This automatically comes with an innate generosity. However, feeling your authentic love for humanity doesn't always come easily or naturally. It begins with loving yourself. If you can truly love and accept yourself then loving others simply becomes an extension of that.

The other prerequisite for generosity is a feeling of abundance. If you subconsciously feel the opposite – that there are shortages – you will develop fears around availability (that there isn't enough to go around), and you will probably find it difficult to be truly generous of spirit. So, look at your attitudes towards abundance. What might be impeding your belief in it? Does it come from somewhere in your childhood? Or does it come from hurt? We've all felt hurt in our lives, but do you have unresolved hurts in your life? This might make it harder to both trust and love. Perhaps it's time to resolve those hurts and let go of them.

Flexibility

One quality that will assist you in learning to live with grace is the ability to be flexible in your life. That is, not only to 'go with the flow', but to be able to surrender to whatever it is that existence throws at you. Remember: It's not the reed which resists the most which is the strongest. It's the one which is prepared to bend with the wind.

In Eastern philosophy they talk about being like a hollow bamboo. This means that if you are rigid in your approach it is much easier for you to be broken. But if you are able to bend and be flexible you will become stronger and grow sturdy.

For the majority of men this proves to be too difficult. They believe that they know 'what is right' and they intend to do things their way. They are often fixed and rigid in their approach to situations. But, often, there is a better, more subtle way to deal with things.

Think of a martial arts master. That man will be finely balanced and totally alert in his approach. He will use the energy of his opponent against that opponent and he will allow himself to relax into a situation. If the martial arts master rigidly tried to hit out or defend himself he would find himself at the losing end. You can become that martial arts master in life as you learn to enjoy the dance with life.

There is a tendency for most of us to be controlled by our ego – it is our puppet-master. And our egos are very wily and very clever. If your ego detects the remotest possibility that you're trying to not be controlled by it, then it will cause you to doubt, deny, and disallow any attempt to free you from its control.

But the ego will often also send you mixed messages. For example, your ego will love it that you might consider describing yourself as a god (and by 'yourself' of course the ego is really thinking about *it*self). On the other hand, it will also tell your mind that you couldn't possibly be a god because it has an investment in keeping your self-esteem low. That way it is able to exert more control over you.

A god is gentle when he needs to be gentle, and tough when he needs to be tough. He knows when to allow himself to be vulnerable and when to protect himself. He has a strong sense of his own boundaries and other peoples' boundaries. I've talked a lot in this book about being aware of your own boundaries, but it is also important to be aware of others' boundaries. For example, unless invited, it is not up you to tell your friends how to live their lives. Mutual respect is very important, and the best way to earn respect from others is to show respect to them.

Another form of flexibility is in how you deal with life's 'ups and downs'. Life never runs smoothly in a continuous way (it would probably be incredibly boring if it did). Everybody has their good days and bad days, their 'trials and tribulations' and their celebrations. And also those days where, on the surface, nothing much seems to be happening. We want the good times to last forever and the 'bad' times to just disappear (or for *us* to disappear). And some of those days can be extremely challenging.

However, on the wall in my home I have a quotation (attributed to the author Vivian Greene) that says "Life is not about waiting for the storm to pass, it's about learning to dance in the rain". I need to keep this permanently in front of me because, like most men, I forget this very important message. I forget that that I need to live each moment, however challenging it might be. In fact, it's often in my most testing times that I learn the most about myself.

Which brings us to…..

Trust

Perhaps you might think it strange to list 'trust' as a quality. But, in fact, it is. I'm not specifically talking about trusting others (or even yourself). What we're talking about here is the ability to be in free-flow. That is, partly what I was just talking about with "Life is not about waiting for the storm to pass, it's about learning to dance in the rain". Because you will find that easier to do if you can also learn to trust in existence.

Many communities talk about how the 'right' thing will happen for you at the 'right' time. Or that life or God will provide you with exactly what you need. Of course, the operative word here is 'need', because that often seems to be different from what you think you want. This is a way of saying that a Higher Power knows better than you. You may or may not believe this. The point is to stay in a state of trusting within yourself. The process itself will make you stronger. I understand that if you're facing some kind of adversity in your life then living in trust is difficult (and sometimes feels impossible). But, ultimately, when you've done everything that you can think of to deal with that adversity, all that you really can do is to trust. So it's better to have that trust in your life all along as part of your being and not wait until your last resort.

You can also assist the process of trust by embracing the positives in life rather than the negatives. In fact, one way to attain satisfaction is to want and appreciate exactly what you have (rather than something else).

This can free you from many things. It can remove a great deal of stress from your life and make you more relaxed. It can help you to focus on what you actually need. And it can make you happier.

In fact trust isn't something that you *do*. It's something that you allow to happen. In spite of thousands of years of human warfare,

I believe that trust is actually a natural state for mankind. We *want* to trust. It's just that we have been taught not to.

I'm not talking about a child-like innocence or naivety (although that is, of course, beautiful). I'm talking about the ability to let-go or surrender to the way that life exists. And once you realize that it's only your ego that won't trust (because then it loses control), you will find it easier to allow yourself to simply trust.

4: IS BEING A GOD THE SAME AS BEING A WARRIOR?

> **'If you are to be triumphant over anything, it is your negativity, your ordinariness, your lesser self'**

There is much advice these days telling men to be warriors, and that it will make them more manly. But this 'manly' state that they're talking about isn't relevant or authentic for most men in the twenty-first century. And, in any case, you can go so much higher than that as a god.

Here are some qualities that might define warriors: They are meant to be brave and they're meant to be bold. They are prepared to die for a cause. However, 'being brave' is often only bravado, and the 'boldness' is often only aggression. And being prepared to give your life for a cause is pure conditioning by others.

In fact, I believe that when people talk about being a 'warrior' they actually mean being a god. For example, they might be thinking of a samurai type of warrior: a man who has developed himself to the utmost and is fully in touch with all of what we have been discussing here.

Let's look for a moment at what else is meant by being a warrior. A warrior exists for the sole purpose of winning. "The war must be won!". And, therefore, if you are a winner, then obviously somebody else is going to be a loser.

Life is not about winning and losing. If you are to be triumphant over anything, it is your negativity, your ordinariness, your lesser self. The dictionary definition of a warrior is "being a soldier or a fighter". Do you really want to go through your life fighting about everything? Think how much energy that uses – energy that could be used for your own betterment and for creating positive outcomes. Think about what constantly fighting means in terms of your relationships with others.

And what is the cause that you're fighting for anyway? How necessary is it to fight when you might achieve more by other means? And what happens when the cause itself actually ceases to be important anyway?

Surely there's too much fighting that happens today. We are beset with numerous wars all around the world. Then there are: the War on Terror; the War on Drugs; and not forgetting the Battle of the Sexes. So much of being a 'warrior' appears to be about domineering others and being an alpha male. But a man's need to domineer over others is driven mostly by his insecurity. He lacks trust and, deep in his subconscious, he almost certainly has feelings of inferiority. The only person in the world that you need to master is yourself. Once you have done that, the desire to master anyone else will fall away.

Another reason why some men choose to be fighters is because of their unquenchable anger. So, again, instead of looking inside at what drives him, a warrior externalises his anger and directs it at others. This resolves nothing and only serves to keep a man stuck in the lower realms of his potential. It would be so much better to deal with the anger as soon as you become aware of it. And, as we've already discussed, if you can *be* that anger, ride it out, understand it and discover where it comes from, you can then let it fall away and you can live your life without that anger having power over you.

In another way, being a warrior is also overkill. Like muscle-building gym junkies, it's possible to get distracted from your true course and go off in the wrong direction.

I have read many articles about 'becoming a warrior' that include the words: combat, stealth, sorcery, endless struggle, asceticism, enemies, "freedom in pain" (I kid you not!). These are not words that relate to being a god. They don't even remotely resemble words that pertain to being a god.

There are several reasons why a man might want to be a warrior. For example, the testosterone that courses through the body and mind of a young man might fire up his blood. He might feel ready for a fight, perhaps to prove himself, perhaps simply for the thrill of of the action. This man might also have high ideals about being a warrior. He might identify with the ethos of the samurai. However, while the samurai had codes of conduct, they were, in many cases, simply soldiers doing the bidding of others. Your life is not about doing the bidding of others. It's about self-awareness and self-actualization.

A man might believe that being a warrior is a high ideal, and that it will "make him a man", forgetting that he's already a man. What he needs to find is something that will make him something higher than just a man – a god.

Wanting to be a warrior might also be an over-reaction. Coming from a position of weakness a man might believe that if he were to display the characteristics of being a warrior then he will be respected.

There might be peer pressure in your life. You might feel obliged to take up the challenge to prove something to others – or, indeed, to yourself. However, as Lao Tzu said: "Care about what other people think and you will always be their prisoner". Your freedom comes from being an individual and being true to yourself and your own needs. Peer pressure is one of the worst reasons ever to do anything.

And there's another really bad reason to want to be a warrior (or, in fact, anything at all): you might believe that that's what a woman wants you to be. A man might look around and think he sees warrior-types being very successful with women. Or he might even believe that the woman in his life wants him to be a warrior, that she will feel more protected. She might have actually told him that. The question that man needs to ask himself is: does he want to be with an immature weakling princess who needs a warrior to protect her, or does he want an independent, equal goddess with whom he can soar in life? Of course many women want to be both protected and independent. But what I'm talking about here is how *you* think (and feel) about *you*rself. This whole book is about being a god – not a mere warrior.

How do think of yourself? Do you see yourself as having to fight to get things done? Do you find there are many battles in your life? Are there many causes in your life (real and imagined) that require you to constantly be pugnacious? And, when you "fight the good fight" do you see yourself as a warrior? Because, if it were valid to be a warrior, the best type of warrior would be the one who develops himself and prepares himself for all eventualities, but never actually *has* to fight. Because he will always trust existence and find better ways to deal with situations. The warrior who has to fight has already partly lost the battle.

And, mostly, being a warrior is about aggression. Let's be clear about the distinction between being assertive and being aggressive. Far too few men learn how to be properly assertive. It is not a subject that is taught in schools and, mostly our parents don't teach us either. In fact most of our fathers and forefathers didn't know how to be assertive either, so how could they teach us? In addition, many cultures teach us to be non-assertive – to be pleasers, to surrender our own needs in favour of others. So what happens is that many men will submit and take it (and take it). They will bend and subordinate themselves instead of laying down their boundaries: "This is what I need" or "No, that's not okay for me". Until something happens! And then they react. Or, I should say, *over*react. And, at that point they become aggressive. And then, if they think about it at all, they actually believe that they're being assertive. But they're not, this overreaction is aggression.

A man who is non-assertive with poor boundaries ultimately may become diminished in his own eyes and in the eyes of the people around him. But the man who allows himself to become aggressive, especially when it becomes his modus operandi, is not even fulfilling himself as a man, let alone as a god.

There are some men today who believe that a woman wants them to be 'aggressive'. They think that because the woman enjoys being passive, receptive and 'claimed' that this requires them to be aggressive. But these men have misunderstood. There is no doubt that most women want a man who is strong in his masculinity, a man who is confident, decisive and assertive. But a goddess doesn't want an aggressive warrior. A true goddess wants a god.

There is also a tendency for the 'warriors' of this world to have virtual armour to protect them from their emotions. (This is one reason why they become a warrior in the first place – it's a good distraction from what is really going on.)

The armour that I'm talking about is an *emotional* defence that supposedly prevents a man from being wounded. Often a man will construct this because he is afraid that if he is sensitive or vulnerable he is going to be hurt. He develops this as a boy through the experiences that he has in order to protect himself. The armour shields him from others' remarks, attitudes and behaviour. However, by definition, this 'wall' that a man constructs separates him from others. And it not only keeps others out, it becomes a prison that he is locked inside. With this armour you cannot connect with others properly and you cannot grow, because your armour is rigid and unyielding.

As a god you need to have free access to all your emotions, to be totally in touch with them and how they're driving your thoughts and your actions. It serves you no purpose whatsoever to be out of contact with your emotions.

These are some examples of armour:

You simply avoid being around people (and therefore no-one can hurt you;
- You've adopted an *attitude* of "I don't give a shit what you think" (which is totally different from simply not being controlled by what others think);
- Your first reaction is always anger (this prevents you from actually having to feel anything);
- You always blame others (rather than taking responsibility for your own actions);
- You always need to be in control (of others and the situation);
- You will do anything (including using addictions such as alcohol, drugs and sex) so that you don't have to feel;
- You can never sustain a relationship (because as soon as the relationship becomes too intimate you need to leave. Here I'm not talking about the intimacy of sex. Clearly it's very easy to have sex without intimacy);
- You automatically go on the attack (because attack is the best method of defense).

So, if you have it, be aware of that armour and learn to shed it in your relationships with others and, most importantly, in your self-realization.

5: ON BEING A GOD (WALKING, TALKING, BEING)

> **'A god doesn't need to feel or be defensive about anything'**

"Walk tall, walk straight and look the world right in the eye"

From the song 'Walk Tall' (Lyrics © Shapiro Bernstein & Co. Inc. Writer Don Wayne)

There is something about the bearing of a god – how he carries himself –that is reflected in the words of this old country song.

If you haven't noticed already, your body posture is deeply connected with your emotions. Which also means, on the one hand, how you feel is mirrored in your body posture. And, conversely, your posture will affect how you feel – especially about yourself. If you're feeling afraid or intimidated, or even especially vulnerable, your body will contract and you will physically express protection of yourself. This is a natural phenomenon. And, when you think about it, it makes sense.

Part of the awareness that I wrote about earlier includes checking in with yourself to notice what emotions you're experiencing. I suggest that you do this on a regular basis – not so that you can become self-obsessed, but so that you will know which emotions are driving your actions. Obvious examples are anger, shame, guilt and fear. And once you start becoming aware on a deeper level you will also begin to notice the more subtle emotions.

Next time you check in with what's happening with your emotions become aware also of your body posture. Are your shoulders hunched over? Are your arms crossed over your chest? If you're sitting (especially with others) are your legs crossed. And are they pointing away from the person you're talking with? These are all indicators that your emotions are impacting on your body.

But here's a really important point: you can change how you feel by changing your posture. For example, if you realize that you may be feeling a little fearful, it helps to stand up. If you then straighten your body – so that your head is held high and in alignment with your body – and you breathe deeply and regularly, much of that fearfulness may drop away. You can experiment with this. Try walking with your head slumped and your arms and shoulders hanging down. How does that feel? Like you're beaten by the world? That's right. Not so good is it? Now stand upright, hold your head up and stick your chest out. How does that feel? Much better? Yes. If you want to change how you're feeling try changing your posture and also try standing or walking instead of sitting or lying.

So you can therefore see that your bearing will affect how you feel about yourself. And, if you stand up straight with your legs apart, you will feel stronger and more like the god that you are.

There is a secondary benefit to this as well. Because other people respond to your body posture. Much has been written on this subject. Human beings (and other animals) are always trying to gather information about others in terms of how that person relates to them: Are they friend or foe? Do they love me? Are they angry with me? And so on. One way we gather this information is by body language. This is often very reliable, although human beings tend to gather information about others based on their own projections. If you project into the world an image of being a god then others will respect that and *treat* you as a god. This, in turn, will make you feel more god-like.

So, back to the song: "walk tall, walk straight and look the world right in the eye". In other words, your posture will assist you and your body language will cement that situation.

How you move is a reflection of your inner being. How clear are you about your sense of purpose in the world? Do you know what you want and need? Do you know what will benefit you? Or is there confusion? It is important to have some idea where you would like to be going in life, even as you remain in the present. It is something like driving a car. You need to be completely present (aware and alert to all around you) and, at the same time, be looking ahead of you at where you're going, as well as to events ahead. When you drive, if you were to be only looking at the front of your vehicle – or worse, not concentrating at all – then I guarantee that life would not work out so well for you! You can, of course, change course at any time. And if you do that, do it with awareness as well.

And, when you walk, walk like a god, and walk with a sense of intention. Decide where you're going and go there. Obviously you learnt to walk when you were a child. But the type of walking I'm talking about has a kind of majestic quality to it. In other words, there is purpose in your movement, just as there is purpose in your life. One will reflect the other.

When you are having important conversations with other people (especially the goddess in your life) *be* with them completely. Make an effort to be as present as possible to what they are saying. Take it all in before you respond. Your ego and your emotions may make you want to interrupt the other sometimes. And you may even want to acknowledge what the other is saying by sharing your own experience. But this is by no means always appropriate. Naturally, when you're riffing and just joking around, you won't want to take things too seriously. But, in any situation where someone is trying to tell you something, it is important to be present, to be aware, and to listen with both an open mind and an open heart. Look the other person in the eyes and respond appropriately and naturally to what they are communicating. If you don't understand, wait for an appropriate time and tell them that you don't understand.

Also be alert to what reactions come up in you when they say something. As we've discussed earlier, it would be wise to ask yourself which emotions in you are being triggered. On the negative side, for example, do you feel threatened or misunderstood? When the other person speaks do you feel the need to jump in to defend yourself. Some people fear that they will forget what they were going to say. If you have this fear then, when you know that you're about to have an important conversation, I suggest that you have a pen and paper available. Ask the other if it's okay to make notes and explain the reason (so that you can give them your attention without needing to jump in) and take short and concise notes – try to keep the notes brief so that you can maintain eye contact as much as possible.

Some people hate being interrupted and you might need to ask them if they've said all that they need to say for the time being before you respond. This is because they easily lose their train of thought. There are, of course, some people who will never stop talking. If you just let them talk they will go on forever. But then you have to ask yourself whether you need to continue a conversation with them (and, sometimes, whether you want them in your life at all).

Do your very best to put yourself in the other's place and to try to understand where they're coming from when they're expressing themself, and then assess what they've said. You might not actually like or agree with what they've said, but that's not the point right now. What's important is that they're trying to convey something to you. When they've finished (for the moment) it might be appropriate to double-check with them what you *heard* them say, using some of the same words that they used. (Do NOT simply parrot back to them the same words. This can be intensely annoying. And, in fact, for some people it feels like they haven't been heard at all.)

And, when you speak, speak clearly and concisely. Try to articulate the main points and don't wander off subject. Talking with another person is about communication. When you communicate you are conveying something to them and they are conveying something to you, whether that's information or an emotion. There are two parts to this. Firstly, you need to be clear what it is that you're trying to communicate. If it's something personal about you, you obviously need to speak your truth and you need to express it in ways which are authentic and comfortable for you.

But the second part is this: do you truly want the other person to understand what you're saying? Presuming that you do, you also need to find a common language. And, by that, I don't just mean English or French, for example. I mean that you must find a 'style' of speaking. If you use words and phrases with which the other person isn't familiar then you risk the possibility that they may not understand what you're trying to communicate. In which case you're wasting your breath. If you're simply venting – blurting out something because it's on your mind – then all you're communicating is emotion. It is, of course, okay to express emotion in an emotional way. But be clear within yourself and with the other person what it is that you're doing. For example, you might tell them that you feel emotional, and these are the reasons why…..

If it's a concept that you're trying to convey, keep it simple. Stick to the main points. If you need to describe 'background' keep it as brief as possible. And, again, look them in the eyes and watch their responses. If you feel that they're not understanding what you're saying then double-check that with them.

The big question to ask yourself is why are you saying what you're saying? Are you trying to make a point? Some men seem to think that they have to have an opinion on every subject. This is simply their ego speaking. And they often need to convince other people of their beliefs. The only reason to do this would be if you weren't sure of your own views or beliefs. In which case you may like to have an intelligent back-and-forth discussion. Find out about the other person's views and beliefs. Then get clear in your own mind, and then you won't need to try and foist your beliefs on anyone else.

And, once you begin this process of growth and self-actualization, it is very tempting to begin preaching to other people what you've learnt from other sources. This is what neophytes often do. They almost start thinking of themselves as a guru. You are *not* a guru (and neither am I – not in the western sense of the word), and this is hazardous territory. Beware! If you feel tempted to start preaching to others, learn to listen to yourself. What is it that you're 'sharing' with them? Focus on these thoughts silently and shut up! Because these are lessons for *you* to learn not them. Respect their integrity and the fact that they are responsible for themselves and their own growth.

Or are you answering a question from someone? In which case give them a concise, honest answer. Then ask if you have answered their question. On the other hand, do you feel misunderstood. Many men (myself included) have felt misunderstood in their lifetimes. This is often to do with our relationships with our parents. Do you keep hammering away at the same point, believing that, if you say it often enough (or loud enough) that the other person will 'get it' or get 'you'? And do you feel frustrated when that doesn't seem to happen? Do you also enjoy banging your head against a wall?

At some point you have to realize that the other person either doesn't understand you or doesn't want to understand. If it's the former, then it might not be *what* you're saying. It might be the actual words you're using. Perhaps your terms of reference are different to theirs and you might need to try and define what you mean by certain words or phrases. In this you might be surprised. Even though you've both been brought up speaking the same country language, your understanding of certain words can be vastly different. Also, for example, some people take a literal, pedantic approach to words where others take a more colloquial or nonconformist approach to words. So, if it's important, you must first define your terms (like they do in a written contract). And be aware that other people will interpret what you say to them through their own filters which are based on their experiences, their culture and their upbringing. So you can be saying one thing and the other person interprets your *meaning* as something completely different. It's quite possible, for example, that what you understand when you read my words is not what I meant when I wrote them.

Alternatively, are you feeling defensive about an issue? If you allow yourself to get into a defensive mode you immediately step out of being a god. Because a god doesn't need to feel or be defensive about anything. *You* know why you did or said something. If the other person doesn't understand – or worse, doesn't believe you – <u>that's not *your* problem</u>. As I said earlier, if they ask you to explain something, then explain it. Otherwise, what are you doing? Being defensive in your words is like chasing your own tail. It's a pointless, fruitless act. So, state your case; check that they understand; answer any additional questions; then move on. Asked and answered! Also feel free to ask them why they're asking in the first place and why it's important to them. The answer to this question can be very revealing and can help you to not only understand them, but answer their future questions.

And sometimes it's better to just keep your mouth shut.
Remember: you are a god. Behave like a god. You are answerable to only one person: yourself. It is your responsibility to act as immaculately as possible. It is your responsibility to live your life in the best way you know how, to grow and develop into the god that you are. It is not your responsibility to live anybody else's life for them. And it is not their responsibility to live yours.
Make your home into a temple (to you *and* your goddess) The English word "home" is from the Old English word *hām*, which refers to a place where "souls" are gathered. It is essential that you treat your own home as such. Therefore, the more that you can make your home into a temple to your higher self, the more nourishment you will receive from your home.

And, consider this: your home is a reflection of you. If your home is cluttered, disorganized, and messy, then the chances are that your mind is like that too. If you are holding on to old stuff that is no longer relevant in your life today, then the chances are that you're carrying baggage from the past in your mind.

Your home is meant to nurture you. It is, after all, the place where you spend a large part of your life and a place where you can be at your most vulnerable. If it doesn't nurture you, where are you going to find that nurture? If the energy in your home isn't clear, what effect is that going to have on your personal energy?

So make that place a temple to the god that you are (and for your goddess too). It's time to take a good, hard look at your temple. How sacred is it? How aware are you of whether or not *all* of it nurtures you? There's more to being nurtured than just feeling comfortable. Rather than *just* sustaining you, your home should feed you energy – you should feel refreshed being there. How do you feel when you arrive at your front door? Are you happy to be there? Does it gladden your heart? How conscious are you of how, say, sitting in a particular chair makes you feel? When you walk from one part of your home to another part how does your body feel? Can you move freely without obstruction? Can you easily lay your hand on all items that you need? Is your home organized in a way that makes you more efficient? And, most important of all, can you totally relax your body and your mind? Do you ever change things around just to see how that feels? This is certainly a worthwhile experience, even if you end up just replacing everything as it was.

If you live with others, ensure that you and your goddess (or, indeed, anyone else you live with) are in accord about everything in your home: the décor; the layout; the colour-scheme; a possible theme. Since 'harmony; is the key word in your temple, then there needs to be harmony between you. If there is disagreement try and find a solution which best suits everyone. Be tolerant with each other.

How aesthetically appealing is the décor? Does it lift your spirits or do you really want to half shut your eyes and ignore it? Think of temples that you might have visited or pictures you might have seen. There are generally themes and objects which are placed *just so*. This is for a reason: it keeps the energy clear and pure. And that is exactly what you should be doing in your home.

Many people live amongst too much clutter and disorder. This impacts on their energy both visually and spatially. It is much better to have fewer, well-placed objects than a multitude of 'stuff'. You might like to ask yourself why you have placed objects in your home. Is it to make it more 'homely'? Is it to fill up an empty space (in which case, why do you need to fill up empty spaces)? Again: think about your temple. You wouldn't dump stuff in a religious temple. Why do it in your own personal temple? Try putting some of your things in closets and see whether you miss them or not. Keep putting more and more away until you can strike a balance between the ascetic and the homely. If you haven't missed stuff after a lengthy period of time consider getting rid of it altogether.

Do you have growing plants inside your home? These are important because they will help harmonize your energy just by being around them. However, be sure to remove dead leaves and flowers. That is dead energy that, however subtle, will have an impact on your energy. It can also be useful to place plants in corners to round them out.

Having broken objects around you or light bulbs that don't work may also affect you energetically. This will reflect how you feel about yourself. So try to ensure that everything is always kept in good repair and also that light fittings always have working light bulbs in them.

What is the normal temperature inside your home? For example, many people keep their homes far too hot during the winter. This can stultify your energy – physical, mental, and etheric – and make you sluggish. And, since you want your energy flow to be as near perfect as possible, I suggest that you experiment with various temperatures. Try and feel which temperature makes you feel the most alive.

Choose pictures and objets d'art with care. Make sure they lift your spirits and nourish your Higher Self. The same with colours and with the lighting.

Many people like to take off their shoes before entering their home. They say that, by removing their shoes, they are leaving their concerns and stresses of the world outside of their private space. Experiment, and see if this is true for you. At the very least it will keep your floors cleaner.

Establish a special place in your home which you might like to feel is a meditation space (even if you don't actually meditate). You might like to have cushions here to sit on and a few special objects that you consider sacred. I'm not necessarily talking about religious icons, but objects – both natural and man-made – which hold a special significance for you. This is your altar to you: the god. This can be a focal point where you can come to reinvigorate yourself and regenerate the energy of your Higher Self, where you can always come to feel your god-ness.

6: HOW DO YOU TREAT YOUR BODY, YOUR MIND, AND YOUR EMOTIONS

> **'In order to function at your highest level it is essential to be totally balanced and in harmony within yourself'**

Most people are familiar with the phrase "a healthy mind in a healthy body". If you are an elite athlete you're going to train frequently. You're going to get your head in the right space. And you're going to focus. You're going to keep on learning. You're also going to apply yourself frequently to your endeavour. As a god it is essential that you have the same attitude: That you stay as fit and healthy as you possibly can in both body and mind. Like anything else, if you want to obtain peak performance you have to maintain your resources at the highest level possible.

And it's not only about *maintaining* your resources. For a god it's necessary to go one step further. What does it mean when we say: "The body is a temple"? it means that you have been given this amazing vehicle in which to live your life. So treat it like that; treat it with respect, nurture it, and maintain it to the best of your ability. Your body deserves nothing less. And, literally, treat your body as a holy entity. For example, when you wash yourself in the shower or the bath don't just scrub away mindlessly with the soap for a few minutes, care for your body with reverence – bathe yourself with love, affection and devotion for this body. This is not vanity, this is appreciation for what you've been given.

Take the time to be aware of every part of your skin's surface. Feel whether it's rough or smooth. Notice the variations in colour. There are no straight lines on a human body, so experience the various curves. Touch yourself with a combination of making an offering to a god (which is actually what you're doing) and the ways you would stroke a lover with whom you're deeply in love. And don't just clean yourself, *cleanse* yourself. There is a world of difference in these similar words.

Imagine for a moment that someone gave you a magnificent and very valuable racehorse. I bet that you would want to care for that horse as best you can (if, for no other reason, than that it might win money for you!). You would make sure that the racehorse has the best quality and best balanced diet – and the correct amounts. You would make sure that the horse kept fit by having regular training sessions and also by allowing it occasionally to run free. You would make sure that it always had prompt and thorough medical supervision and treatment. And you would ensure that its stables were kept clean, comfortable and at the correct temperature. You would also ensure that the horse had a happy and contented life, because then it would serve you well.

I'm sure you've seen where I'm going with this. I'm sure you can see that if you would do all that for an animal, certainly you would do the same (or better) for yourself.

Do you feel comfortable in your body? If not, why not? Is it something about the shape or the size of your body? Are you concerned about your height? Are there parts of your body that you don't like? Do you feel uncoordinated? Does your body feel awkward – almost as though you're moving about in someone else's body? Becoming more familiar with your body may help you. Take some time on a regular basis to find a few minutes in a quiet space to stretch the various groups of muscles in your body. As you do so, bring your awareness to each muscle. Feel the energy there and feel how that muscle supports your body and its functions. Note that I am not talking about general exercise. These are exercises to become more familiar with your body. (In addition there's a good chance that the tense/relax exercise at the end of this book may also help.)

An admission: I hate exercise just for the sake of it. I have tried going regularly to the gym. I used to be a runner and played football when I was younger and I trained regularly for those activities. But I hated even that. I found it boring and lacking in enjoyment. So I found ways of exercising that suit me. I like to dance, swim and go for walks. These are my preferred methods of exercising my body. And, apart from driving, I also never sit down for long periods of time. I get up and move my body. I do the same on airplanes. I keep my circulation moving freely and do stretches and gently exercise my muscles.

The challenge for you is to find something that you enjoy. Something that you can keep doing. And something that will keep you active, fit, and healthy.

But whatever forms of exercise you choose, do it to be 'in it' (not 'out of it'). Do it consciously with compassion for your body.

This is a way of nurturing your body. It will support you now and for the rest of your life. (And it will probably healthily extend your life.) Be clear, especially if you're doing gym work) that you're not doing anything that punishes your body. 'No pain, no gain' does not belong here. Also mix it up a bit. Find techniques that will improve your cardiovascular system and something that focuses on your muscular system.

These days many men enjoy yoga. It can be an excellent form of exercise because it stretches you in the right places and it can bring you peace, harmony and balance. If you do it properly it works not just on the body, but on the mind as well – which is an added bonus.

Being healthy and fit will help you to *feel* more like a god. And it's something which is within your control.

There is one aspect of health that few people think about in this context. Many people might consider this a joke, but I assure you it isn't: If you are constipated it will sap your energy. It is, literally, an energy blockage. If you can become completely free of constipation it will release a large amount of available energy. And it will also allow your energy to flow through you more smoothly. Constipation will also literally affect whether you are centred or not. It will impact on your centre of balance. And, of course, constipation can also bring headaches which, in turn, will prevent you from being fully focused.

Another area which is seldom thought about is the stress that a misaligned spine can place on the body. If you have a misalignment (or vertebral subluxation as chiropractors call it) that means that your whole body will be out of balance. It might be only slight or it might be more pronounced, but it will be putting stress on your body that will be taking some of your energy; energy that you could be utilizing better. Can you imagine an electric fan that is out of balance and is not rotating properly? It will not be functioning at its optimum. The end result would be true for you.

Also within your control is your diet. I've found more advice on the internet about this subject than just about anything else. And so much of this 'advice' is contradictory. In the end it's tempting to just go "To hell with it, I'll go and have a burger".

The fact is that most of healthy eating is obvious – at least to many people. But let's run through some basics. (Although you might disagree with me.)

If you drive a car I'm sure that you want it to run at its optimum performance capability. As part of that you're going to fill it with the best *and most appropriate* fuel. Obviously you're not going to overfill it, nor are you going to let it run dry.

We have many reasons to eat food but the primary reason is as fuel: in order to keep our bodies operating. And, therefore, naturally, you will want to choose the correct food to keep you running as efficiently as possible. In doing this you will look at the various food groups that you need to consume: proteins; carbohydrates; fats; vitamins & minerals.. Your body needs all of these foods, and it's your choice how much of each group you use and which food you eat that constitutes that group. So balance is very important. Not enough protein may cause you to have less energy. Too many carbs may cause you to become overweight. The wrong kind of fats may cause various organs to work inefficiently. This isn't a book about diets. Nor am I about to get into the vegetarian versus whole meat-eating argument. That is up to you. However, it is essential that you get to feel what *your* body requires.

There is reliable research which shows that there are connections between your stomach and your brain – that there is, in fact, an information exchange between your brain and your gut. Firstly, it's obvious that if your stomach is upset then that will prevent you from thinking as clearly as you might. But, in addition to that, in trying to solve 'problems' your brain will borrow energy from your gut. This is especially true if your mind is stressed. What happens then is a retardation of the flow of mucus and blood required for proper digestion. This will weaken your gut walls and, eventually, have a deleterious effect on the immune cells that live in the gut walls. This then becomes a circular problem, with brain impacting gut and vice versa.

There are two points to this: firstly, it's important that you eat in as a relaxed a way as possible in order to give the maximum energy to your digestive system. And, secondly, that you consume healthy, nourishing and digestible food.

Equally important is the frequency and quantity of food that you consume. Portion sizes in the developed world are often excessive. Most people eat far *too much* food for their systems. I suggest that you think about precisely how much your body needs. Try gradually cutting down the quantity to find out how much food is enough *for you* without being too much. Also consider stopping eating before you feel full. The point is to feel satisfied, not stuffed. Putting too much oil in the engine of your car is not going to make it run better. In fact not only is it wasteful, but it's likely to actually damage the engine.

Many people also eat too quickly without even considering what they're consuming. Try eating slowly with small mouthfuls, savouring each mouthful as you go. (I sometimes eat with a teaspoon. This forces me to take smaller mouthfuls.) Appreciate and enjoy your food as you present it as an offering to the god that is you. Make it a meditation, because this food not only nourishes your body, it can also nourish your mind and even your soul. Be grateful for the sustenance. Be grateful for the quality and selection of food available to you.

It's also important to vary what you eat. Even if you have the same basic dish every day, try and vary the ingredients. It is healthier for your digestion and also helps to keep food interesting for you. And the more interesting it is, the more you can savour it.

You can also make food preparation part of your meditation. It used to be that a lot of men were useless in the kitchen. That isn't true today. We have become inspired. So get into the kitchen when you can. Delight in the creativity of cooking food. (And you could also take pleasure in preparing something for your goddess.)

But your body is just one part of you. Equally essential is your mind. When you have control over your mind you have control over your life. It is vitally important to keep your mind active and clear. Not only will you function better with a strong mind, but you will live a healthier, longer life. Your mind is the key to your emotions, which in turn impact on decision-making, relationships and interactions, sense of self, and simply 'being'. That is why your mind requires as much nurture as your body. So, similarly, you need to feed your mind, you need to exercise it, and you need to be constantly aware of its state.

Clarity of mind is, of course, essential for your awareness and your perceptions. Those brain synapses need to keep happening like a well-oiled machine.

In prehistoric times, when men were out hunting, they needed to be aware and alert at all times, not just to catch their prey, but to make sure they didn't end up as prey for something else. The modern era seems to provide for fewer opportunities to exercise our brains. Also, today there are more and more gadgets that can actually stop us from using our minds, and instead we are pushing buttons, swiping or clicking. And we do these things mindlessly. We also rely on politicians, religious leaders and corporations to make our decisions for us. And, if we watch television or spend our time on social media, we are passive consumers. All of this turns our minds to mush. Which is how those who want to manipulate us like it. Because that makes us more controllable and manageable.

But, as a god, you certainly don't want to be controlled or managed. You want to be free to make your own decisions about what is right for *you*.

So, in terms of feeding your mind, think about what goes into it. How do you feed *your* mind? Do you have stimulating conversations and discussions with others, where you listen to each other and absorb information? Do you test your mind and stretch it to take in new information? Do you take time to think about subjects – really think things through? For example, do you look at both sides of an argument? Do you imagine subjects from others' perspectives? Do you think about *your* truth?

Or do you stick with what's familiar and easy? Do you stick with your beliefs, which stem from what others have told you, and do you maintain those beliefs throughout your life without ever questioning them?

Do you read stimulating books and quality, balanced newspapers and journals to keep you abreast of what is happening?

All of these can be used to keep our minds active and alert.

The relationship between the brain and the mind is similar to the relationship between a computer's hardware and software. They function together. And the more you use your brain, the more you will also be exercising your mind. So it's important to use your mind as much as possible. Once upon a time we used to do mental arithmetic. This was actually necessary in daily life, and it kept our brains alert and alive. Today, even for the most simple calculations, we rely on machines. Even when driving, we used to have to think about where we were going, but today we rely on a GPS.

Therefore, what we need to do is to find different exercises to activate our minds. There are many simple methods: puzzles like

Sudoku; quiz and trivia games; and numerous mind exercises which can be accessed (somewhat ironically) on the internet.

One underrated mental exercise is to write. Many people believe that a piece of writing needs to be for someone else. But it needn't be the case. Challenge yourself to write a description of an event or an object. Write about how you're feeling or an experience that you've had. The latter can also be cathartic and help you to get in contact better with your emotions. And writing generally, especially when it taxes your brain, is a very healthy activity. And write primarily for yourself – for your own clarity and your own wellbeing. That is an end in itself. If you feel like letting someone else read what you've written, then that is entirely up to you. However, if you do that, be clear in yourself. Don't let someone else's opinion of your writing affect how you feel about the writing. And, especially, don't let it affect how you feel about *yourself*.

Just as your body needs to relax and be refreshed, so your mind also needs to relax and be refreshed. There are various techniques to assist with this. Best of all is some form of meditation. As not all techniques appeal to every man, I suggest that you find a meditation that suits you best. You might like mindfulness or vipassana. Or something less rigid like yoga nidra might appeal. And, since it's basically about quieting the mind, simply sitting or lying undistracted and allowing calming music to flow around you may assist in refreshing your mind.

It is virtually impossible for most people to actually stop all thoughts. So, when you're practicing one of these techniques and you're aware of a stray thought, don't judge yourself. Just notice that "there's a thought" and gently bring yourself back to the technique. Here's a way that helps some people: Imagine a completely blue sky. The thought is like a small cloud crossing. Just allow the cloud to cross until the sky is all blue again.

In your life, most of the time it's important for you to be totally in control of your mind. But in these instances you're not actually trying to control your mind, rather it's the opposite. You are surrendering to bathing and refreshing your mind.

What does a god wear?

Whatever makes him feel like a god. Experiment with colours, and style. I know a man who feels more like a god when he wears tighter clothing. I wear a lot of black because I feel more in my power when I do that. In my experience there are some people who react when others wear black. But that is for them to process. The point is that I feel more in my power. This is not arrogance or lack of caring for others. Simply that I refuse to give my power away because somebody might react badly.

Stress Management

As we've already discussed, to fully embody your god-ness you need to be functioning efficiently and effectively. However, something that will prevent you from doing that is stress.

A certain amount of stress is essential in our lives. Without it our bodies would not work properly. Stress is defined as 'a measure of tension'. And both our skeletal systems and our muscle systems rely on tension, just as tension is what keeps bridges up.

However, the type of stress that we're concerned with is an excess of that tension, so that we're stretched in ways that are not conducive to healthy living. Too much tension causes anxiety, lack of awareness, and the inability to fulfil our true purpose.

It's now known that when an individual is experiencing chronic stress, then Cortisol is released into the system. And elevated cortisol levels interfere with memory and learning. They lower immune function and bone density, increase blood pressure and cholesterol, cause weight gain, and heart disease. Chronic stress and elevated cortisol levels also increase risk for depression, mental illness, and lower life expectancy.

If you are feeling anxious or even 'just a little stressed', your thinking is going to be affected. Therefore your perception and your awareness are not going to be as efficient as they could be. You will interpret situations through a filter; the decisions based on those perceptions will not be the best decisions, and the actions you take will not serve you as well, and you will not be acting optimally.

If you constantly have too much stress in your life this will begin to impact on your autonomic nervous system, and this in turn will have a major effect on your physiology. Epinephrine is a hormone that is secreted in your body when your central nervous system is stimulated in response to stressors such as anger or fear. It increases your heart rate, blood pressure and cardiac output. The theory is that it was important to have all those increases in prehistoric times when threatened by a vicious creature, because the increases would help us if we chose either to fight the creature or chose to run away (the so-called "fight or flight syndrome"). But, of course, today our chances of being threatened by a vicious creature are few. So what happens is that we just have elevated heart rate, blood pressure and cardiac output, without doing much about it. And too much of that will kill you.

It is, therefore, essential to manage your levels of stress. The important word here is 'manage', because even if you wanted to try and eliminate all stress it would be impossible. The best that you can do (and actually need to do) is to *manage* your stress.

As always, the first step in handling a situation is to recognize that there *is* a situation. Become aware of when you are experiencing stress. What are your symptoms? Are there changes in your body? Does your mind behave differently? Do you interact with other people in a different way?

When you become aware of feeling extra tension or stress look at what it is that is causing you to feel that way: your stressors. These stressors do not, in themselves, *make* you stressed. In fact it is your reaction to them that causes you to feel stressed. I'll repeat that because it is very important to comprehend: Things in themselves do not cause you stress. It is *your reaction* to those things that causes you to feel stressed. These stressors trigger something in you – often mostly in the mind – to which you react. And it's that reaction – *your* reaction – which causes the stress.

So, your mission is, firstly, to determine what those triggers are. What, precisely, are you reacting to? A simple example might be that you're running late for a meeting. Your mind will be running through all the various consequences of you being late. Psychologists call this Mindtalk. At that time you are not focussed 100% on what you are doing because your mind is playing out various *future* scenarios.

Here's a little story to demonstrate how Mindtalk works: John and Mary have just moved into a new house. John can see that his lawn needs mowing, but he doesn't own a lawnmower, nor does he have the money to buy one right now. He has seen a neighbour using a very expensive-looking lawnmower, but he's never spoken with this neighbour. He decides to ask the neighbour if he can borrow the machine. But, as he's walking up the street, his Mindtalk begins to kick in. It says "This guy doesn't know me. Why would he lend it to me? And, besides, it looks very expensive, he's not going to lend it to a complete stranger,". By the time John reaches the neighbour's house he has worked himself into a lather of negativity. When the neighbour opens his front door John says to him "I didn't want to borrow your lawnmower anyway". And John walks away. (Of course, it's a joke. But that's how the mind actually works sometimes.)

Of course he would have been much better not projecting what the outcome would be. And the same is true about you guessing or projecting what someone thinks about you.

When you have identified your triggers you will then be in a position to do something about how you respond to them. Notice I'm not saying *react* to them. It is your choice as to whether your response is a reaction or not. You could, in fact, choose not to react. You might simply note that you're running late and, instead of worrying about the consequences, simply focus on where you are right now.

The American theologian Reinhold Niebuhr famously authored what is known as the Serenity Prayer: "God grant me the serenity to accept the things I cannot change, the courage to change the things I can, and the wisdom to know the difference."

You can apply that advice to all the stress triggers in your life. Can I do something about this? Yes? No? If No, then I must simply accept it and focus on what I *can* do. An example of this might be someone who gets stressed by the events they see when they passively watch the news on television. There are some truly awful things that happen in the world. Some of them we might feel like we can do something about. We might, for example, donate money to starving children. But there are other events which we often feel impotent to affect. The frustration that this can cause might bring about a high level of stress. In this case you must accept that there is nothing you can do and leave it at that. Alternatively you might decide to not watch the news at all, and take a more proactive course in obtaining your news information. It is therefore up to you to decide what you can or can't change.

There are other times when our chattering minds cause us stress. Often the mind will project the negative – whether that's what someone thinks about us or an outcome to an event.

Another source of excess stress is time management. Sometimes this comes from trying to cram in too many activities and sometimes it comes from poor organization. Either way it would be good to look at your life and see for yourself whether you get stressed because of time. If this happens to you, are *you* trying to do too much. In this case you need to prioritize your activities. Make a list, from the most important to the least important. What can you lose from the least important activities that will improve your stress levels?

If your problem is poor time management then you will have to impose some discipline on yourself. It also helps to draw up a *realistic* time schedule and *stick to it*. Enlist the help of your family and friends if you need to. And you can do this together with prioritisation. You can also look at whether you procrastinate. If you do, it's time to look deeply at that. Why do you do it? Is it an unpleasant task? Are you unhappy with what you have to do? Is there something else you'd rather be doing? Do you feel that you can't do something as well as you'd like? Are you doing something as a favour rather than being true to yourself? It might be time to stop doing whatever it is and change your life.

Also learn to be realistic with your time planning. For example, if you're driving somewhere and you know that you've parked your car some distance from where you live, allow the time to walk to the car and prepare to drive off. And, of course, build into your time-planning possible delays.

Sometimes our finances are huge triggers for stress. And, often, we give more energy to worrying about finances than doing something about it. I know it's easy to say, but worrying will not help you! It truly won't. In fact, not only will it cause you more stress, it will make you *less* likely to do something practical to help.

It is incredibly important to address the cause of your financial issues as promptly and as thoroughly as possible. Work out a plan for how to increase your income and/or how to lower your expenses. If you owe money to anyone don't hide your problems –

from others or yourself. Go and sit down with them and work out a re-payment plan. Most people are reasonable. If they can see that you're not ignoring the problem and that you're making an effort then they will help you. After all, it's in their interests to do that. And maintain regular contact – even if you feel embarrassed because you can't make a re-payment. Remember that what really upsets people is when you owe them money but they never hear from you.

If you have multiple debts it's often a good idea to take professional advice, which might include consolidating your debts.

And if you just can't help worrying, here's an idea: give yourself a Worry Hour. Say to yourself that between (say) 5.00pm and 6.00pm every day is your Worry Hour. For the other 23 hours you can say "I'll worry about that at 5.00pm. I don't need to do it now".

How are you currently dealing with your stress? Do you feel like you need to use alcohol and/or drugs? Do you zone out with mindless activities? Do you take it out on others? None of these is actually addressing the situation. It is far better to remove unwanted stress from your life altogether. Then you can live a healthier life.

There are various courses of action that you can take when you become aware of unwanted stress. The first, as I've said is to be aware of your Mindtalk and to address that. You can also channel your stress into positive activities. For some people that might mean a form of exercise. For others it might be socialising more. If you have the time and resources, it might mean having a project to work on that will take your mind off the triggers to which you are reacting.

The primary – and best – stress management technique is to breathe! It's astonishing how we fail to breathe properly when we experience stress. We breathe shallowly, too fast and too high in our chests. So, when you're feeling stress, the first thing is to look at your breathing patterns. Slow your breathing down and deepen it. Inhale for 4 seconds and hold it briefly. Then exhale and hold it again for 5 seconds. As you do this, try to breathe into your belly, rather than the top of your chest. Then, as you continue breathing, try gently extending the periods of time. Do this for a few minutes and you will begin to feel less stressed and more relaxed. You will then be in a better position to focus on your Mindtalk and focus on what the triggers are that you're reacting to.

There may be times in your life when you simply feel overwhelmed by events. All of your life might seem to be in a tangle. One thing seems to impact on another until it's all too much to deal with. A process you can employ at these times is 'chunking'. In other words, breaking down problems into small, workable tasks. You might want to take some time to sit down and write a list of all of your problems (knowing that you're about to find a way to resolve each of them as soon as possible). Be clear that, in each case, you don't have to identify with the 'problem'. And that it is not a burden to carry on your back, but a puzzle to be solved. Above all, remember that you do not need to make yourself a victim or a hostage to your problems.

Forgetting all but one of your problems, take that one and see whether you can, in fact, break that down into smaller components. And, looking at the components, brainstorm and write down a list of possible solutions. (You can do this alone or with others). Don't judge any of the possible solutions at this time.

If you feel too closely identified with a problem you could try thinking of it as a problem that a friend might have. What possible solutions might you offer them? And what advice would you give them?

Lists, generally, are very good for stress management. As well as listing all your 'problems' so you can chunk them, writing To Do lists or shopping lists can help, just as keeping a calendar for forthcoming events or diarising your activities can also assist your memory, and therefore take pressure off your mind.

Physical touch also helps greatly in managing your stress. Even if you're not in a relationship, it's important to have physical contact. A relaxation massage can work wonders on a temporary basis. Hugging and being held also increase the levels of various hormones and chemicals into your system. Your body releases oxytocin when you cuddle, especially with someone whom you're close to, Cuddling also releases endorphins, (hormones secreted within the brain and nervous system which have various physiological functions. They are peptides which activate the body's opiate receptors, creating a calming effect).

Are you the sort of man who 'burns the candle at both ends'? Do you get enough sleep? Alternatively, are you getting too much sleep? You may already be aware whether or not you're getting not only the right amount of sleep, but also the right quality of sleep. If not, take yourself to a quiet corner, close your eyes and try to feel whether your nightly sleeps are nourishing you enough. If you're often feeling tired and/or sluggish you are certainly not going to be the god that you could be. You may need to adjust your sleeping patterns, the room lighting, or your breathing. You may even not be aware of suffering from sleep apnoea or blocked sinuses. If you believe this to be the case, check it out with your doctor.

I wrote earlier about being a pleaser and being *in*authentic. A part of not being true to yourself is when you are constantly trying to satisfy others. And that in itself can be very stressful. It can feel like trying to fill a bottomless pit or feed a constantly hungry child. This can either be because the person (or people) you are trying to please never allow you to relax or because something inside of you believes that you are never fully satisfying them.

For a great many men the latter began in our childhoods. We might have had a parent or an influential teacher, say, who never let us feel as though we had pleased them. Whatever we did was either not good enough or never adequate. So, ultimately, what we're trying to do today is really only the small boy inside of us trying to please that person. And that's why we experience stress. Because we're actually attempting to fulfil something from the past – not the present.

Instead of being a pleaser you might, conversely, have a big "fuck you!" to the world. It often seems as though people you meet are 'idiots', and many of your interactions with others end in anger displays. Although you might attempt to shrug off these exchanges, you know in your heart of hearts that, not only are they stressful, but they can be avoided. There are many, varied, reasons why your life is like this. But, as far as this book is concerned, you should make it a priority to look into why it happens because, ultimately, it will prevent you from fully realizing your god-ness.

In terms of stress management don't undervalue simply doing nothing. We appear to live such busy lives these days, with multiple distractions, stimulations, and inputs. How often do you give yourself the opportunity to just do nothing? To simply be, without the need to look at or listen to something? I'll bet it's very rarely.

In his book *In Praise of Idleness* the British philosopher Bertrand Russell wrote "Like most of my generation, I was brought up on the saying: 'Satan finds some mischief for idle hands to do.' Being a highly virtuous child, I believed all that I was told, and acquired a conscience which has kept me working hard down to the present moment".

Or, consider what the Welsh poet W. H. Davies, in his poem "Leisure", wrote:

"…A poor life this if, full of care,
We have no time to stand and stare".

In other words, occasionally, Don't Just Do Something. Sit There.

To summarize: In order to function at your highest level it is essential to be totally balanced and in harmony within yourself. If your level of stress is too high you will not be able to do this. That is why it is important to manage your stress.

7: REALIZING YOUR FULL POTENTIAL

> **'You were born full of potential. That's all you were when you were born'**

I'm sure you're familiar with the phrase: 'being on top of your game'. Well, how about if you could be on top of your game for the majority, if not all, the time? How would that feel? Most men would say "yes, I'd like that". But others might find the proposition intimidating, because then there's a "what then" situation. In other words, "if I was like that all the time I'd actually have to perform and I don't believe that I could do that. I might fail". So they sabotage themselves. They create a life and a lifestyle where they are mostly sub-par. Subconsciously this then gives them an excuse to not have to try most of the time.

But what if you told yourself that you could be on top of your game most or all of the time and then you didn't actually have to *do anything*? All you had to do was feel good. All you had to do was 'be' without any expectations from you or anyone else. How would that be for you?

When you were born it was as though you were told "Here is your life. Here is your destiny, go and fulfill it. The question is: have you heard the voice that said that and did you listen to it?

You were born full of potential. That's all you were when you were born. Your whole life was ahead of you and what happened to you after that determined what you would do and who you would be. The influences and various impacts made you the man you are today. But have you realized yet all of the potential that you were born with? What did you dream of when you were a child? When you were a teenager how did you want your life to be when you became an adult? How has that worked out for you? In your heart of hearts do you feel that your destiny has been fulfilled yet? Do you have more in you? If you honestly believe that you have actually realized your full potential, that this is it, well fine. There's no more to say. But even if you have an inkling that there's more in you, then it's time to bring that to life.

"Know Thyself" was written at the entry to the sacred oracle of the Temple of Apollo at Delphi. It was there to remind all men of the most fundamental element of self-discovery, because you cannot truly make any important decision about anything in your life without self-knowledge. It is the rock upon which you build your life. Know *why* you do what you do. Be in touch with all your emotions. Notice your thoughts and your thought patterns. See your influences. Really look at all that you consider your shortcomings and see whether that is true (whether they *are* shortcomings) – and, if so, why. See all your successes and triumphs in life for what they are. Understand your part in your relationships (without focusing on the other's actions). Examine your beliefs.

THE GOD THAT YOU ARE

A god knows what he wants and he aims for it. He prepares a clear picture and focuses. He will use every tool within his command to empower himself.

What would you say is your potential? What might you achieve in life? How much can you grow throughout your lifetime? What is your role in society? *Who* could you be?

It's time to look deeply inside of you without any kind of judgment. What do you believe you are capable of? Are you putting limits on yourself? And, if so, where do these limits come from? Because, ultimately, these limits are obviously restricting, and they will prevent you from realizing your full potential.

You may well be a man who believes that he is capable of *anything*. But most men are not like that. Since they were children they might have been told by their parents, their siblings, their teachers, their peers and by society that there are things they either cannot or should not do. Is this you? If you were to be completely honest with yourself what is it that you believe you're capable of? Have you ever found yourself saying "I couldn't do that". Or worse "I shouldn't do that". Ask yourself where that belief comes from. Is it because of something that you've been told? Is it something that you've tried once and felt that that you didn't succeed, so you gave up?

It's time to get real with yourself. If you knew that you were going to die tomorrow what regrets might you have about things you never did or never tried to do? How would you feel about the way in which you lived your life and aspects you didn't change, even though you could have?

In your heart of hearts what would you *really* like to do? What would you like to be? So, what is stopping you? What is *really* stopping you?

Actually, I'm not talking about what you'd like to *do*. In point of fact I'm talking about how you'd like to *be* or what you can be.

What is your potential? Can you continue to grow and develop as a human being in terms of your consciousness, your spiritual evolution, and your awareness – both personal and general? Or have you simply given up? Have you decided that "That's as far as I'm going. Any further is too hard"? If so, I urge you to reconsider. As far as I'm concerned, I believe that I will keep learning and developing until the very last second that I live. And you can be the same.

The secret is in being open: Open-minded and Open-hearted. If you remain open to possibilities and potentials from within yourself and from outside of you, you will continue to develop. If you learn to surrender to existence your journey may be joyful; or at times it might be painful; it may even be boring. But, if you stay open, I promise you that you will continue to learn and to develop. And you will inhabit your potential.

You may not, in fact, have been told that there are things you cannot do and ways you cannot be. You might have been told that you can do or be anything, but don't know where to start. There are too many choices. Almost too *much* potential. So, where to start? Firstly consider where you're at in life right now. Are there aspects of your life which you feel are not serving you well? These might include your lifestyle, your job, and your relationships, or even your attitudes. If there is something that you honestly feel you should change, then change it. Yes, it really is as simple as that. (Be aware, I'm not saying it's always easy. I'm saying it's simple.) Make the decision and trust that you will be alright. Because now it's time to move on with the rest of your life.

Having relieved yourself of aspects of your life which you feel are not serving you well, allow yourself to feel the void that is often created. This can be quite a scary time. Certainly the Unknown creates fear in us. But know that nature abhors a vacuum. And where you're about to go in your life is going to be exciting and rewarding. There may be challenges, but any challenges will only serve to inform, if not strengthen, you.

Now it's time to consider what you want. Sketch out in your mind (or even on paper) the broad strokes of what would fulfil you. Not just now, but way into the future. What would give meaning to your life? For example, many men decide that they want to serve the community in some way. Or they feel they would like to make their mark, or have some great achievement in their life. Or they want to improve the quality of their life. What are your priorities? What is top of your list? It's time to be that man.

And, remember, being a god is not about trying to be something you're not. On the contrary, it's about allowing yourself to be something *you already are*.

Build up your inner core strength. Ensure that you stay healthy in body, mind and spirit so that you start from a position of strength. Resolve to stay strong and be as aware as you can be of anything that takes away your strength. If you begin to feel disturbed or unsettled feel those emotions that bring that about. Process those emotions and look at the thoughts behind the emotions. What is your Mindtalk? Mostly, by understanding your thoughts (and therefore your emotions) you will be able, in time, to eliminate any sense of being unsettled.

Knowing who you are will contribute greatly to your inner core strength. You will therefore come from a position of confidence. This will not only assist in centring you, it will in turn inspire other people, who will then enhance your sense of confidence.

Having a strong inner core will also help you deal with the situations that come up in your life and also with your relationships. And dealing with these in an appropriate manner will, again, feed back into further developing your inner core strength.

All of these will assist you in realizing your full potential.

How have you been living your life up to now? Are there things in your life – and ways that you behave – that you do without thinking? And have they become habits? It's time to be conscious of your habits and to examine them. For simplicity's sake let's divide them into 'good' habits and 'bad' habits. Which of all of these would you say are serving you well?

A good habit will contribute to your wellbeing in some way, whether that has to do with the food that you eat, the money that you save, the way in which you handle relationships, or the way you do your work. It is just as essential to develop good habits as it is to get rid of bad habits.

A bad habit is simply repeatedly behaving in an unconscious way which is detrimental to your wellbeing. A part of you has made a decision not to act consciously, either because you don't care enough, or perhaps you don't have enough time, or because you have given up. A bad habit does not serve you as an integrated man and it certainly doesn't serve you as a god.

A good habit will mean that, for example, you always put your keys in the same place so that you don't have to hunt for them, waste time and get stressed. A bad habit may impact on your health, cause you to lose friends, or have additional repercussions which impact on other areas of your life.

It's now time to look at all of your habits. Ask yourself how the good ones are working for you. Do they need to be refined? You may want to change them occasionally just to keep you aware.

More importantly, it's essential that you become fully aware of your bad habits. And here you might even like to engage the assistance of your family and friends. (Although, be aware that it's them who are considering these habits 'bad'. Because, on reflection, you may not actually consider them bad habits yourself). What do you do unthinkingly that, ultimately, is not good for you?

Once you've become aware of your bad habits you have to make a decision to change them in some way, either by mitigating them or by eliminating them altogether. Make a note to check back in with yourself after a period of time – perhaps one month – to ensure that you have, in fact, changed them.

When you have changed your bad habits you will be in a much better position to fulfil your potential.

Many men are afraid to stretch themselves because they are afraid of 'failure'. This is interesting. What exactly does 'failure' mean, and why is it important? Obviously it means that you have not achieved the outcome that you set out to attain. But, so what! Why does that carry such a stigma? What is it about 'failing' in other peoples' eyes (or even in our own eyes) that carries such intense energy? All that is happening is that you set out to accomplish something and it didn't work out exactly the way you wanted. This happens to scientists in their laboratories all the time. For artists it is part of their daily experience. But so many men, when they don't accomplish something precisely as they expected, almost curl up and die with shame. And it cripples them! It makes them afraid of attempting *anything* because they're afraid of 'failure'. And it starts when we're very young. Most small boys will have a go. But the reaction that we get from parents, teachers and other boys and girls means that we stop making those attempts because we learn that mistakes are 'bad'. In fact they're part of the process of learning, of creating, and of developing ourselves.

Every time a teacher marks a test with a lower mark and comments in a negative way, he is not teaching you about 'succeeding', he is actually teaching you to not try. Every time a parent makes a derogatory remark about your endeavour, they are indoctrinating you to believe that you are somehow lesser because of the level of your success. (And it's worth pointing out that there *are* often *levels* of success and there is always something to be gained and lessons to be learned from your endeavour)

And then there's *Star Wars*' Yoda who famously said "Try not. Do or do not. There is no try". In context what he actually meant was "Don't attempt something half-heartedly". But generations of men have taken in the quotation and have said to themselves "Okay, well I won't bother to try then". And, if anything, that 'not trying' is, itself, the real failure.

Also, attempting something marks you out from the herd, whether it's climbing a mountain or creating a work of art. Men often feel that they want to make themselves 'small targets' so that they will not experience derision from others if they don't 'succeed'.

But what is it that makes a man a 'success'? So many of the 'successful' men in the world actually failed until they finally succeeded. Each time they failed they learned something and applied it to their next attempt. And they took risks. Because sometimes you just have to.

It's not just about doing, of course. It's also about being. You might have had ambitions when you were younger that you have given up on. Often this is because of peer pressure. You might have fallen victim to one of the many negative expressions in modern parlance: that you were a 'try-hard'; 'overly ambitious'; or a 'wannabe'. It's very easy for this to happen. People who catch crabs at the beach know that when they catch them they can put them in a bucket and they do not need to cover the bucket. This is because when one crab tries to escape from the bucket the other crabs will pull it back inside. You might have experienced the same syndrome.

So don't be afraid to fail. In fact, give yourself permission to 'fail'. The experience itself will enrich you – regardless of the outcome. And, if nothing else, you will find out for yourself what your actual potential is.

What inspires you in life? Is it certain people? And precisely why do they inspire you? Is it because of what they do or the way in which they do it? Is it something about their personality? Hopefully it's not just because of their 'fame' (or infamy). Do you aspire to do what they do or be how they are? If so, I suggest that you let them inspire you, but achieve your own potential in your own unique way.

What other things inspire you in life? I have known inspiration to come from many sources, including animals. The Scottish writer Sir Walter Scott in 'Tales of a Grandfather' wrote about Robert the Bruce. He was a hunted man and took refuge in a small cave. As he sat there he watched a spider trying to make a web. Time and again the spider fell and then climbed slowly back up to try again. Eventually the spider managed to stick a strand of silk to the cave wall and began to weave a web. This inspired Robert the Bruce, and he went on to defeat the English at the Battle of Bannockburn. Sir Walter Scott wrote "If at first you don't succeed - try, try again."

Look around you. What fills you with wonder? Take this wonder and use it as a source of energy in your own life. Many creative people I know draw inspiration from other creative sources outside their own discipline. In other words, whatever it takes to get your juices flowing.

In addition to your desire, you will need to maintain self-discipline, determination, focus and commitment to realize your potential. How strong is your commitment? It is essential to be absolutely clear within yourself as to what you want to do or how you want to be. Keeping a journal can aid you with this. Many people also like to keep a Vision Board, where they post pictures and words that keep them on track.

Sharing your journey with others can also strengthen your resolve. But remember to check in with yourself from time to time that you're sticking to *your* journey and not someone else's agenda.

Find your gifts. In business they talk about your USP (Unique Selling Proposition). Theodore Levitt - a professor at Harvard Business School - stated that "Differentiation is one of the most important strategic and tactical activities in which companies must constantly engage." The same is true of all gods. In the movie '*The Life of* Brian' Brian exhorted us to acknowledge that we're all individuals. While you might share your godliness, you will have your own unique qualities. What special gifts do you have? It's time to find those gifts and work them to realize your *full* potential. You might be surprised: your potential might actually be bigger than you thought it was.

And, at the end of the day, find what it is that makes you feel strong in yourself, and do that. Be aware how much vitality you have and how you feel. If you feel week when you're involved with certain activities or with certain people, then you know that this is not the correct path for you. And, on the contrary, if you feel strong when you're involved with other activities or with other people, then you know that this is how you should be living.

8: ACCEPT YOURSELF, ACCEPT YOURSELF, ACCEPT YOURSELF

> **'Your level of self-esteem is fundamental to how you fully realize your god-ness'**

Yes, I can't say it enough: Accept yourself. Accept who you are. Accept your strengths. Accept your weaknesses. Accept your abilities, Accept your (perceived) limitations. Accept your influences. Accept your penis size. Accept your IQ. Accept your cultural background. Accept yourself. And, really, if you don't accept yourself, how do you expect others to accept you.

That doesn't mean give up. And it doesn't mean that you can't improve yourself in many different ways. What it means is that you are who you are. And, as such, you are worthy of love, respect and acknowledgement. Not just by others but, especially, by *yourself*. You are not lesser or greater than another man. Do not compare yourself to others. Let them be themselves. It is your journey (and your challenge) to fully be yourself.

And your journey begins with accepting whom you are right now. This is the material that you have to work with. So start by examining that material in a non-judgmental way. Be as honest with yourself as possible, and start from there.

Embodying your god-ness is about how you see yourself and about how you inhabit that state. But, because of negative reinforcement in our lives, accepting oneself can often be one of the hardest things to do. But you can do it. Just like that!

In the Zen Buddhist tradition they created paradoxical anecdotes or riddles called koans which seemed to have no solution. They were used to demonstrate the inadequacy of logical reasoning and provoke enlightenment. Seemingly nonsensical, their purpose was to circumvent the mind to teach in a no-mind way.

There is an old Zen koan about a man who put a gosling in a bottle. He fed the gosling and cared for it until it grew into a goose. The koan questioner asks "How is it possible to get the goose out of the bottle without breaking the bottle or harming the goose?" The answer to this question is "The goose is out". As simple as that! The goose is out.

And, it's just as simple for you to accept yourself. You simply decide "Okay, I will accept myself". There are no qualifications. You make decisions: "I will not judge myself. I will understand myself. I will treat myself with respect. I will value myself. I am a beautiful, unique god and I accept myself." (And, if it doesn't feel right at first, fake it until you make it. It *will* become real for you after a while.)

That's not to say that there aren't things that you might want to improve and develop in yourself. But you do that with love and care. Anything can be improved. That doesn't mean that you don't esteem it in the first place.

The American psychotherapist Abraham Maslow claimed that in order to reach the most highly developed state of consciousness, realizing his greatest potential (being a god), a man not only needed to discover his true purpose in life, he also needed to pursue it. However, before he could take that path, certain needs had to be met. In laying this out he created a pyramid-like structure which he called a Hierarchy of Needs. He stated there are seven layers, and only once a layer had been met could a man devote time and energy to dealing with the next layer. He divided the seven layers into two blocks. The first four he called the 'deficiency needs'. The top three he called the 'growth needs'. The deficiency needs are absolutely essential before a person can progress to the growth needs. For example, taking care of having enough to eat, etc would be prioritized before being concerned about an occupation. And having good health and security are prioritized before being concerned about intimacy. However, you can also see that having good self-esteem is fundamental before being concerned about the Growth Needs..

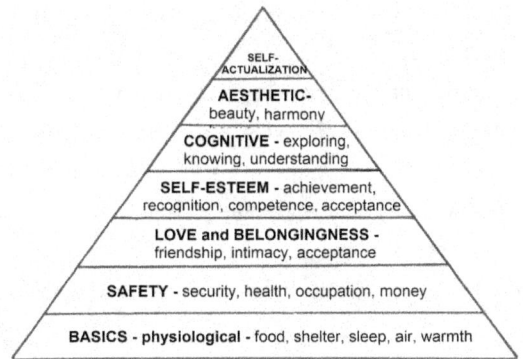

Your level of self-esteem is fundamental to how fully you realize your god-ness. The first step is being aware of your current level of self-esteem. And, in that, being completely honest with yourself. How much do you really believe that you are worthy? Come on: this is just between you and you right now. You don't need to admit it to anyone else. Do you always behave with absolute confidence? If not, why not? What is it that prevents you from behaving with absolute confidence? Can you walk into a room and have no worries whatsoever? If someone else tells you that you deserve something do you believe them 100%? If not, why not? Can you nominate yourself for something (a position, or an award)? If not, why not? Do you believe that you could have that girl, that job? If not, why not? What are your reservations about? Is there self-doubt? And is that self-doubt connected to feelings of self-worth?

Or do you over-compensate? Do you find yourself bragging or boasting? Do you feel the need to dominate (or, more especially, domineer)? Ask yourself why. Is it fundamentally because you actually *don't* believe in yourself?

Once you've become aware that you do have issues around self-esteem the next step is to ask yourself why. Why don't you deserve that job? Why don't you deserve love and admiration? Why shouldn't you be the centre of attention? What is it about you that makes you less worthy than someone else? What inhibits you and makes you pull back?

Most of us carry certain baggage with us in life. There's stuff to do with our childhoods. There's stuff to do with relationships. There are events that happen to us in life which cause distress, trauma and psychological damage. These things can affect us greatly, and we go on dragging this baggage around with us into our current lives; our current relationships; and our current behaviour.

When you look at your self-esteem and notice any areas where it's not as strong as it might be, can you see whether any of these areas have been impacted by this baggage? Have there been any specific events in your life that now cause you to not be who you really are? Do you therefore doubt yourself?

Shame, guilt or regret are common for most of us. But these are emotions which you can acknowledge and be aware of, but not allow them to control your life. They serve no purpose to you whatsoever, and if you can work on eliminating them from your life you will be the stronger for it. Also, if there is someone about whom you feel guilty, your feeling of guilt serves *them* no purpose either. Do something practical instead. The trick is to acknowledge whatever you feel shame or guilt for (or regret) without letting it control you. If there's something you haven't done or said and you feel guilty about that, either do or say it and then let it go. If you've done something or said something which you're inclined to feel guilty about, it is far better to do something useful about it instead. You could apologise or make amends in some way. Recognize the event, honour it, and then drop it. It doesn't need to control you now. It certainly doesn't need to affect your self-esteem. That's all easy to say, I know. But it really can be as easy as that. It's up to you. If you make the firm decision to drop it any time it comes up, it will eventually fall away by itself.

You can certainly learn from the experience and let it guide you in the future. This is an opportunity for you to grow into the god that you are.

The question is why do you want to have any feelings of shame, guilt or regret? Does this sound like a strange question? Well, there are many reasons. For example, there's something called 'secondary gain'. This is something which you might not be consciously aware of. It's actually an advantage that you might receive, such as increased attention from others or being released from responsibilities. In this case it might mean that you feel that you don't have to put in maximum effort. So your tricky mind will stop you (subconsciously, of course) from dropping your shame, guilt or regret because they give you an excuse not to have to commit yourself 100%.

One other reason why we hang onto shame, guilt or regret is that they've become habits. We do them unconsciously and automatically. We don't examine those feelings. This is partly because we've actually been taught to have these feelings: if you do wrong by someone, then you should feel guilty about it or you should be ashamed. Why? It is possible, as I say, to acknowledge the action and then move on. You might have hurt someone. Well, apologise and move on. You might have done something which, in retrospect was a mistake. Recognize it (and learn from it) and then move on.

If you believe that shame (in particular) is driving your life because of something that was done to you, - maybe when you were a child – I strongly suggest that you work with a professional counsellor such as a trained psychologist to process the shame so that it no longer is in control.

(In the workshops that I run about shame we talk about the snowball effect, where you keep adding shame to your life. We also work on dis-identifying with our shame.)

A god acknowledges his responsibilities and his role within society. He is empathetic and sympathetic. He has a moral sense of right and wrong and he is concerned with human welfare. These are all positive aspects. Shame, guilt and regret are not. They are negative aspects and will simply affect your self-esteem and cause you to not be who you could be.

A part of accepting yourself is loving yourself. Many men have been told that this is actually a 'bad' thing. I'm not sure if there could be anything more twisted than that. If you don't already, it's crucial that you learn to appreciate and love yourself.

I'm not talking here about narcissism or being self-obsessed and self-centred. This is not "it's all about me". This is about loving yourself as you would love your goddess. It's about valuing yourself, having compassion for yourself, being kind to yourself, nurturing yourself, being completely non-judgmental and loving yourself unconditionally. Why do so many men find that so difficult? After all, if there isn't love in your heart for yourself, is there truly love there for someone else?

The key to loving yourself is understanding yourself and having compassion for *you*. Do you feel that you have unconditional love for someone else, whether that's a parent, a child or your beloved. What does that feel like? Is your heart open to them simply because they exist? Do you sometimes get irritated by things they do, but you still love them? Do you find that you are able to forgive them and then move on with your lives? Do you simply accept that this is who they are, and it really doesn't affect your love for them? This is how you need to behave with yourself.

Even though you're a god you're not always going to get things right 100% of the time – not in your own eyes anyway. So, occasionally you might feel like you make mistakes! Some mistakes are small and some can be very big. So what! Rather than blaming yourself because you're not perfect, it is far better to understand what happened, why you did what you did? Learn from the experience and apply it to the rest of your life. Forgive yourself. Don't blame yourself. Blame is negative energy that prevents you from acting optimally. Don't play the Blame Game – with yourself or anyone else.

It's possible that you don't believe that you are worthy of love (from yourself or, indeed, from anyone else). Many men feel it to be true for them. You need to go deep into yourself and see whether this is true for you. If it is your truth, it's very important that you look at this and examine why it's so. There's an excellent chance that it came from your childhood. It might be necessary for you to work with a professional counsellor (for example, a psychologist) to examine why you don't believe that you are worthy of love.

Many of us have been taught from a very young age that loving oneself is vanity, selfishness, and *very bad*. We were taught to always put others first and not to focus on ourselves. But, again, I'm not talking here about being narcissistic. There's room to consider yourself *and* others. I particularly wrote it that way round: consider yourself. And then consider others. Do you have a reaction to that? Look at that reaction. Why would it bother you so much? Because you're meant to be altruistic? Because you're meant to be unselfish? Because you're not meant to think about yourself?

Do you feel that you have undesirable aspects to your character or undesirable traits? And do you believe that these traits make you less worthy of love – especially loving yourself? Firstly, look at that belief. Why would character traits make you not worthy of love? These traits are part of the authentic *you* right now. You might choose to change them in the future. But, for better or for worse, that's who you are. It's time to accept and love that imperfect being just as you are.

Secondly, who told you that these are undesirable traits? Do you base your feelings of self-worth and self-esteem on what others have told you about yourself? Was it someone else or does it come from you? Exactly whose values and ideals are you using to judge yourself against? Are the values and ideals undesirable based on legal, cultural or religious norms? How do you really feel about them? If, in your heart of hearts, you're actually comfortable with these aspects of you, then why would you judge them to be unacceptable?

This is important stuff. It's fundamental not only to you being a god, but also contributes to your level of happiness. Because, if you're always judging yourself and criticizing yourself, you're not going to be a very happy person. This will affect other people who will then reflect it back onto you. So tackle it *now*.

If it turns out that you're not actually comfortable with these aspects of you, then change them. If you're doing something that you don't feel is right, then stop it. Do it differently or do something else. And remember to love the *you* that's making the change.

THE GOD THAT YOU ARE

Love this you that is learning life's lessons and is growing and developing.

Are you the type of man who tends to focus on the negative? Do you often look at what's 'wrong' rather than what's 'right'? Now would be a very good time to see whether you're applying this to yourself. Are you inclined to be more aware of your failings? Whether you do that or not, it would be far better to be compassionate towards yourself.

As you begin to fully have compassion yourself and to fully accept yourself, you will gain more confidence in yourself. You will also develop more assertiveness. This confidence and assertiveness (not aggressiveness) will be attractive to others and, when you become aware of that, it will in turn assist you in accepting and loving yourself more. (Note that the opposite is also true: the less you accept and love yourself the more likely you will be to attract to you people who will abuse you and abuse your trust.) People tend to believe what you believe about yourself.

When you feel insecure you may react to situations and towards others in ways which are not in your (or their) best interests. And you may behave in ways which are not authentic.

Know who you are. Not in relation to a woman (or, in fact, to another man). Know who YOU are. Know your capabilities and your failings and come to terms with them both. Work on them if you choose, but come to terms with them. Because when you come to terms with them it really doesn't matter what anyone else thinks of you or says about you. And, if you truly come to terms with them, your self-respect will increase.

There is one more thing on this subject. Feeling unlovable can also create a sense of insecurity. The more unlovable you feel the less secure you're likely to feel. This can create something of a vicious circle as the insecurity feeds into the need to prove that you're worthy of being loved – either by others or by themselves. Many men believe this. They believe that they have to *do* something that makes them worthy. Again I would pose the same question: if you have someone in your life whom you love do they need to prove that they're worthy of being loved? The answer should be 'no'. They simply *are*, and for that you love them. So drop any idea that you have to prove anything. Just be yourself – the god that you are – and that is enough.

9: THE GOD AND HIS GODDESS

> **'Hold your goddess in your life like you would hold that which is the most precious imaginable to you'**

The yin yang meaning and symbol (also known as the Tai Chi or Taiqi) date back to ancient China and represent the belief that everything in the universe consists of two forces that are opposing but complementary.

According to yin yang philosophy, the universe and everything in it is both constant, cyclical and balanced. One force dominates and then it is replaced by the opposing force. This activity continues constantly and repeats itself over time. Illustrations of this philosophy of yin yang include Life and Death, Darkness and Light, and Night and Day.

These apparently opposite or contrary forces are actually complementary, interconnected, and interdependent in the natural world, and they give rise to each other as they interrelate with one another. They form a dynamic system in which the whole is greater than the assembled parts. And, as you can see, one cannot exist without the other.

The symbol also represents the Divine Masculine and the Divine Feminine. Traditionally the black area represents yin with the following characteristics: The feminine; passiveness; intuition; submission; softness; stillness; the Moon; darkness; and the night. The white area represents the yang with the following characteristics: the masculine; logic; light; the Sun; dominance; strength; heat; and hardness.

The height of god-realization is when the energy of the Divine Masculine meets the energy of the Divine Feminine, both within you and in relationship with your goddess. And, therefore, the yin yang symbol is a perfect representation of this.

When the masculine in *you* meets the feminine in *you*.

Take a look at those traditional attributes, and you will see that the black qualities don't belong exclusively to women. And neither do the white qualities belong exclusively to men. Although it is fair to say that you, as a god, are likely to possess more of the yang features and in greater strength.

THE GOD THAT YOU ARE

Unquestionably you should build on your yang qualities. However, in addition, in order to be a fully-rounded human being, let alone a god, it will pay you also to enhance the yin aspects of your being. Develop your intuition, allow yourself to be soft and vulnerable (when it's appropriate), and know when to surrender. These yin qualities will complement the yang qualities within you.

Nevertheless, however much you embrace the yin facets of you, it is unlikely that your full life development can proceed to its optimum entirely from inside yourself and without the convergence with your beloved goddess - there will always be a limit to how much you can grow entirely by yourself.

It is the nature of things for a heterosexual god to share his life with a goddess. I'm not talking about having someone in your life to 'complete you'. You are complete in yourself. However, it is the complementary nature of the union, the synergy (when there is the interaction of two or more agents or forces, so that their combined effect is greater than the sum of their individual effects), which will allow you to truly fulfil your journey in becoming the god that you are.

A god will ideally be with a goddess who not only knows herself to be a goddess, but also loves, knows and respects her god, just as you love, know and respect her. Of course the ideal partnership will be when both of you are on the same path, each developing themselves, supporting each other in that endeavour.

This is not a book about relationships (other than the one that you have with yourself). However, since you can transform each other's lives, it is in both your interests to establish a healthy, loving, and growing relationship. So, here are a few things that you can do to engender that.

- Frequent clear communication is absolutely essential in any type of relationship – especially one of this nature. Right from the beginning you both need to establish your desires for the relationship as well as honouring one another as gods. As you listen carefully to each other in turn be very clear and unambiguous in describing your individual and mutual paths. Many couples have a special place where they can communicate. It is away from any distractions, offers harmony, and is not linked to any other activity, such as eating, making love or watching television. Talk about things as they come up (rather than waiting and building up a list of things).

Even with the best will in the world we sometimes do not hear what our partners are trying to tell us. This can come about for many reasons – either because we filter the message through our previous experience; because one is not articulating well enough; because of the fear of the possible consequences of totally expressing ourselves; by tuning out at a critical moment; or the simple fact that we occasionally understand things differently. Allow for this possibility and, if misunderstandings arise, take responsibility for the misunderstanding, honour the new communication, make any adjustments necessary, and move on without blame.

- Dedicate yourselves to the relationship, knowing that it will be mutually supportive and will provide a foundation which will nurture you both as you both become fully realized.
- Acknowledge that you are *both* gods and that this is a sacred union of gods.
- Be absolutely honest with one another. If either of you has reservations of any kind, then discuss these. (Remember that, if she has any, your goddess' reservations are *her* reservations. There is no need to justify yourself or be defensive. Again: these are *her* thoughts and feelings but, if it feels appropriate for you to act on what she has told you, then take that action). Take note of what she has told you and let her know that you've taken note. If you have reservations yourself, sit with those thoughts for a while and think them through thoroughly. If you feel the need to urgently share them,

explain the stage that you're at, and that at this stage any reservations are not fully thought through.

- Dedicate your love-making to the sacred union. The highest and most refined form of sexual blending together of your divine masculine with her divine feminine is tantric sex. The Sanskrit word "Tantra" means woven together, and this form of love-making celebrates you both as divinities. Of course, this doesn't mean that you can't also have lust, fun and playfulness. On the contrary, the more three-dimensional and exploratory the nature of your love-making, the more your relationship will grow. And the more you will grow as individuals.
- Keep the sexual energy contained between the two of you. This has nothing to do with jealousy or possessiveness. It isn't even about traditional 'monogamy'. It is because involving others in this part of your connection leaks energy from your devotion to one another and to your union.
- Remember that when you are making love what you are doing is not a release of energy, but the actual creation of something special in each of you and between you. And this honours the gods that you both are.
- And it doesn't always have to be about sex. Maintain frequent physical contact with each other. Small touches and caresses keep your mutual energy together (especially if you are kinaesthetic or physical people). Taking turns in massaging one another allows you to give and receive and stay in harmony.
- It has been said that there are several ways that one prefers to give and receive love from a partner. For example, your goddess might feel most especially loved when you are very attentive to her physically or when she receives small tokens of your love. You, on the other hand, might feel most loved when she declares her love for you verbally or in writing. Together discuss as early as possible in your relationship how you both feel loved and how you express your love.

- Declare and maintain the intention to find special times each day to connect and totally *be* with each other, undistracted and totally focused on one another.
- Find ways to develop other forms of connection between you, such as intuition and extrasensory perception. *Know* one another so that you both become tuned into the same wavelength.
- Learn to dance through life together
- If there have been hurts in your relationship make sure that you each have the opportunity to satisfactorily express them. Tell each other and LISTEN to each other and thoroughly acknowledge the hurt. THEN MOVE ON. Don't keep dragging the hurts along with you.

In relationships it's tempting to project what someone else is thinking, especially if they're not particularly forthcoming in expressing what they're feeling. We attempt to 'fill in the gaps' of our knowledge, based on hints, clues and past information. The problem is that these data may present an untrue (or, at best, incomplete) state of affairs. Even when someone actually tells us what's going on with them we still pass that information through the filter of our own mind. And, when we process the information, it's coloured by our past experiences (including traumas) and our current mindset. So what you think you hear someone say may, in fact, not be what they actually said – or meant. That's why, when it's important, it's a good idea to check back with the person that you understood what they meant when they told you something. This will help you avoid miscommunication.

You can learn from each other. Just as your goddess will benefit from being with you, so you can gain much understanding from her. Don't let your ego get in the way. Apart from your divine beings, you are both bringing experience and knowledge to the other. I promise you that there will definitely be many aspects of life that she can teach you. Be prepared to absorb that.

If you don't currently have a goddess in your life, there's a very good chance that applying the elements of this book will draw her to you. Keep your heart open and allow for that possibility. In the meantime you could have an agreement with a particular woman that you will play the god role in her life and she will play the goddess role. There is a great deal that you can achieve in this way, even if your relationship is non-sexual.

I have also personally had the experience of manifesting a goddess in my life. I meditated on how I would like her to be, what qualities she would have and how our relating would be. I wrote all of this down and had a small ceremony where I asked for this woman to come into my life. Then I focused on other areas of my life. A short time later my goddess materialized. And I will be forever grateful for that.

Sometimes, when we are in relationships, there is a temptation to try and manipulate another's actions or feelings. Obviously there are times when there is something that you want to do and your goddess might not be interested. The first thing to look at is do you necessarily have to share this experience with her. Certainly shared positive experiences cement a relationship and bring couples closer together. But is it always the case that you need to do the same things together? You are, after all, two individuals, and you may have separate interests. It is perfectly natural for you to sometimes participate in different activities. You will not be losing her if she doesn't join you in something or you do not join her in something. BUT check with her and be really clear with one another. How important is it to her that you join her – and why? And, likewise, exactly why might you need her to do what you're doing. Having separate interests brings air and life to a relationship. It allows you both to be whole gods that you can then bring to one another.

Even more important is to look at whether you are attempting to manipulate her feelings about you or whether you feel that she is attempting to manipulate your feelings about her. The need to control and manipulate others comes from fear — the fear that we will 'lose' the other, and the fear that we will 'lose' the relationship. Occasionally this manipulation is overt but, often, it's more subtle.

There is a type of 'manipulation' that is not really strategic; it comes more from a place of love. Sometimes it might be as simple as you wearing a particular shirt when you go out with her because you know she likes you in that shirt. Or when she touches you in a particular way because she knows that opens your heart to her. I'm not talking about these activities. But there is a more pernicious form of manipulation: the playing of controlling hidden games that have ulterior motives. This kind of manipulation is not only inauthentic, but actually harmful. It also disrespects the gods that you both are. Examples of this might be if she behaves with another man in a particular way to try to make you jealous. Or if you attempt to shift blame onto her to try and make her feel guilty. All this is inelegant, unworthy and damaging behaviour. If you're tempted to do it, ask yourself why. Isn't there a better, cleaner and clearer way to communicate? Look deep inside you. In your earlier life have you been taught by someone that it is necessary to manipulate others?

If you feel that this is the only way you can get something you want, then you have a problem. Either *you* need more skills or the communication between you both is blocked. (In which case you need to ask yourself why that communication is blocked) Or, perhaps, this is not the right goddess for you. In any event, before you try to seriously manipulate your goddess, it would be far better to share with her that this is what you were tempted to do.

Likewise, if you feel that she is trying to manipulate you, then tell her. Not in an aggressive way. Simply say "When you do …..(whatever it is) I feel that you're trying to manipulate me and I don't want either of us to do that". Be clear with her that she can ask you for anything. You reserve the right to be true to yourself, of course, but you will always do your best to give her what she wants.

The challenge of many relationships is that they can become dead, lifeless arrangements. The relating between you and your goddess should be a living, breathing dance, where both of you are present and each moment is new. This is, after all, a meeting of divinities where there is a balance with both of you applying maximum diligence and, at the same time, keeping the energy between you light and playful, and with you always allowing a sense of humour to remain alive. Remember that there is a distinction between being 'sincere' and being 'serious'. The latter is a synonym for 'gravity', and gravity has a heavy, ponderous quality that will sink you to your lowest point. Whereas sincerity means that you honour and respect one another totally and are profoundly available and present to each other.

Hold your goddess in your life like you would hold that which is the most precious imaginable to you. Hold her securely, but not too tightly, with reverence, with delight and wonder, with joy and pleasure. And, likewise, allow yourself to be revered by her for *what* you are and *who* you are. You are precious to her too, and you need to accept that and be grateful for it.

At the same time be careful not to crush this relating with inflexibility. It is possible to become too dependant on others and on the relationship. Always be clear in yourself who *you* are bringing to the meeting of your two souls. Be aware of your own energy and how it meets and complements her energy. The biggest gift that you can give your beloved is to truly, totally be yourself. Don't try and mold yourself in any way just to please her.

    Be strong and decisive in your connections with your goddess. Do not be wishy-washy. Telling her "Oh, well, I don't mind. Whatever you want" is not the way a god behaves. Know what you need and what you want (not necessarily the same thing by any means). Be totally clear in yourself and then tell your beloved. Listen carefully to what she says about her needs and wants, then be prepared to make decisions. Sometimes it's necessary in life to make compromises, and the best kind of compromises are where you both get at least some of your needs met, whether by meeting in the middle or by taking it in turns. If you are making concessions do not carry any disappointments or grudges into the future. It would be better to walk away now than to carry negative energy into the future.

    Be prepared to lead the way. Here is something that you can discuss with your Beloved and establish whether it is true for her or not: When soldiers move through the jungle as a team they have a 'Point Man'. Not only does he have a sense of direction in terms of where the team is heading, he holds the welfare of the whole team and is alert to all possibilities. Think of yourself as 'Point Man' of a two-person team. Your direction will serve you both.

    Your goddess is not necessarily looking for you as a god to dominate her, but she does need you to be master of yourself and to be clear in yourself.

10: HOW CAN I BELIEVE THAT I AM A GOD

> **'Get out of your own way. The only thing that will prevent you from being a god is *you*'**

Some men have said that it is arrogant to think of themselves as gods. However, arrogance would mean that you have *too* great a sense of your own importance. I'm suggesting that you just accept who you are. And who you are is definitely essential to how you live your life.

There may still be a little thought nagging away at you while you read all this: "I still don't actually believe that I'm a god". The questions I have for you are: Is it the word 'god' that is bothering you? Or do you still not accept that you have the potential to totally be a god?

If it's the word, and it truly bothers you, and it's the only thing standing in your way, then by all means find your own word. My dictionary has several meanings of the word 'god', from "a superhuman being" to "a greatly admired or influential person". If it's the 'superhuman' definition that bothers you, that you think that you have to be a able to fly or have extreme physical strength, that is not what I'm talking about.

In fact I don't use it in either of those senses. My meaning is clear: being the god that you are is allowing yourself to be the maximum that you can possibly be.

And when I say 'allow' I mean that it shouldn't require effort. In fact it takes more effort to keep yourself being less than a god. You really have to work hard at that; to find distractions and excuses why you shouldn't fulfil your promise; to justify being mediocre. It is so much easier to just let go into your god-ness.

If you become influential or greatly admired by others, well that's great. But, again, that's not the object of this exercise. The intention is that first you become "greatly admired" in your *own* eyes. Because that will help you to realize your full potential.

If you still don't accept that you have the potential to totally be a god, then that is another issue. You may say, of course, that *nobody* has the ability to be a god. And if, after reading this book and meditating on its meaning, you still believe that nobody has the ability to be a god, then that is your prerogative and your choice.

However, if you actually believe that other men have the ability to be a god, but you don't, then you have a serious issue which requires analysis. We've already talked about self-esteem. Do you perhaps have a low opinion of yourself? Do you compare yourself unfavourably to others? Do you feel unworthy? Have you accepted these thoughts and feelings so that now they've become your reality? Well, I challenge you to turn these thoughts and feelings on their head, because you are at least as worthy as the next man, you have as many rights as the next man, and you are at least as capable in your own way as the next man. I can state all of this without qualification because *all* men have these strengths. Note:

I'm not saying that you are superior to others, but you're definitely NOT inferior.

Or have you just settled into your mediocrity? Does it feel comfortable, like sitting in an old, reassuring armchair? Does it feel as though this way of life is easy and you feel no need to change it, because that would be too 'difficult'? Is that really how you want to live the rest of your life, as a mediocrity? OK, well that's your choice. Good luck with that.

Alternatively you might feel that you would have to change your life, and that is scary. I understand that. Making changes in our lives can feel threatening. And you might say to yourself "Half a loaf is better than none, so I'll just stick with my half a loaf". In this case it would be a good idea for you to look at what changes you think you'd have to make. And exactly what it is about these changes that you find confronting? Do you believe that you'd have to *do* something extra in your life which is irrevocable and feels, in some way, life-threatening?

There are certainly times in our lives when we know we need to make changes, but the changes feel like great leaps into the unknown. And it's quite natural for there to be fear about the unknown. If this is the case with you perhaps you might consider making small changes incrementally.

And all you have to do to commence (without even making any changes) is to accept the proposition that you are, in fact, a god. That's not so difficult is it? Once you can really accept that, then you can begin to act like that god that you are.

Or do you feel that somehow it's your 'lot' in life to *not* be a god? This is slightly different from feeling that you don't have the right to be a god. Somehow or other you have convinced yourself that there is a status quo which cannot be changed. I applaud your surrender, but in this case I believe that it is misplaced. There is, in fact, a big difference between 'letting go' and 'giving in', although it's a subtle difference. The point is that you (and the rest of the world) are constantly changing – constantly in a state of flux. You have only to look around you at the natural world to see how things evolve from one form to another; from one way of being to another way of being. Therefore, you too can evolve. You don't have to be stuck in this place. You can evolve into understanding and self-actualization..

Or do you believe that you could never do what it takes? You may believe it, but couldn't act on it. Again, I would say take small steps. Taking on what might seem like a whole new personality definitely challenges some men. So don't think of it as having to take on a whole new personality. Think of it as a process where you are in transition of *becoming* a god. And if you do truly believe the premise then, whenever something in your life occurs with which you're not one hundred percent comfortable, say to yourself "I am a god". That's all, nothing more. And you will be surprised at the difference.

You actually owe it to civilization to fully realize your god-ness. If there is a purpose in life I believe it is for each of us separately and together to evolve in terms of understanding and awareness. We are all linked through the universal consciousness. And, as one person develops and evolves, they influence the rest of mankind. You have only to look back at the history of civilization to see that. The knowledge that we now possess has been passed down from one generation to the next. Even wisdom (which is very different from knowledge) manages to spread from one person to another. So, the more knowledge and wisdom that you are able to garner, the more you will ultimately profit the rest of the world. We proceed together like a great, ungainly procession moving towards our ultimate destiny of understanding.

When you fully inhabit your god-ness you will influence other men to do the same. Therefore your development is not only self-caring, it is the epitome of altruism.

And, as to the question "How can I believe that I am a god?", you just can. Think of all the information that you currently accept without question from social media. Think of all the beliefs that you've inherited from teachers, parents, friends, and others. You heard it or read it and you instantly believed it.

Know that I'm not asking you to just accept something just because *I* say it's the truth. I'm asking you to question the proposition. I'm asking you to think it through. I'm asking you to allow it as a possibility. It's okay to have doubts. But I do ask you to *feel* whether it's your truth. A lot of men are not good at this. What they know is what they know. And that is driven only by their minds, and behind their mind is their ego. So tell your ego to have a little holiday, allow yourself to enter a meditative space and *feel* whether this could be your truth. I believe you will find that it is.

I know that ultimately you will be able to accept your god-ness. And I know that you will be able to *be* that god. So get out of your own way. The only thing that will prevent you from being a god is *you*.

11: REMEMBERING THAT I'M A GOD

> **'It is simply enough to tell people "I know the truth about myself".'**

Having read this far you may well agree that you are, in fact, a god. You may decide to apply yourself to that, and also clear out all the potential blocks. However, remembering that you are a god could be a different matter, especially during times of stress and high emotion – probably the times when you most need to remember the fact.

Of course, as always, practise makes perfect. In other words, the more times that you acknowledge your god-ness, the more you will remember. So here are a few things that you can do to help you remember during those crucial times. (And don't just remember to be a god, remember to behave as a god does.)

Are there particular circumstances in which you forget that you're a god? For example, in interactions with other people. And do you find these situations have a habit of repeating themselves, perhaps not identically, but similarly? Maybe you get caught up in your emotions. Maybe you have established patterns – certain ways of dealing with situations. You find that you become a baser, more unaware man. What is happening for you at these times? Are you reacting from some period of time or even some specific occasion in your past, possibly even your childhood?

This is when you need to, firstly, really observe what's happening in that moment. And this observation requires you to develop the observer or witness part of you. This is a neutral, completely non-judgmental part, that simply notes what is happening. You can say to yourself "I see this happening". Sometimes you might say "I see this happening *again*. But the 'again' carries no condemnation.

You can practise developing the observer or witness at any time. At any given moment, whether you're with others or alone, you can ask yourself "what are my thoughts right now?" or "what are my emotions right now?". You may be surprised by the responses. Again, don't judge what comes up. Simply say to yourself "Oh, so I'm thinking or feeling that. I see that."

The next step is to try getting in touch with that observer or witness the next time you find that you're behaving less than godlike. At that point don't become disappointed or judgmental. Just see it.

You might feel that you need to take a step back, especially in interactions with others. Don't forget that others too have *their* behaviour patterns. So be clear about not getting caught in their patterns. It is your responsibility to look at how you behave, and adjust that if necessary.

When you take a step back, see where you're coming from in those moments. For example, have you been trying to convince someone of something, are you defending or trying to justify yourself? Or is this just an automatic reflex action? If this interaction has caused you to be anything other than godlike, then immediately drop those motives. Say to yourself "I am a god and I don't need to react in this way. I can choose to behave differently."

Look carefully at what the stimuli had been to bring about your reaction and be on the lookout for those stimuli another time. If you do that, you can then, to some extent, prepare yourself. Don't go looking for trouble. But at least be aware that "This is the type of situation where, in the past, I've forgotten my god-ness. I will be clearer this time about what I'm thinking, how I'm feeling, and where my responses are coming from. And I will remember that I am a god and it's my choice about how I respond to the situation."

Here are a few things that might help you with remembering:

- I talked earlier about establishing a special place in your home. Think of this space also as (literally) the seat of your power. When you are seated here (it doesn't have to be cross-legged; make yourself as comfortable as you can) you can feel the energy moving through your body. Feel it strongly in the soles and heels of your feet, then let it rise up your legs and thighs. Focus on this force as it pauses for a moment around the area of your perineum and then fills your testicles and, especially the base of your penis. Breathe slowly and deeply as you distinctly feel the energy flooding this whole area. Then, when you're ready, let the energy start to rise again, filling your belly and then your chest. Pause again to really feel your heart opening and accepting all of who you are and everything around you. As the energy rises again through your throat, your face, and the rest of your head, (without judgment) see that your mind is now bright and clear. Breathe, and allow that beautiful power as it finds its way to the top of your head as you feel simultaneously the god that you are and at one with the universe. Keep breathing and feel the energy again rising from your feet to the top of your head.

You may choose to have a small ceremony when you do this, perhaps light a candle, burn some incense (not too close to your nose and mouth). Even ring a small bell (sound is very good for many men to assist with remembering).

A mantra is a word, a phrase or a sound that comes from the Hindu and Buddhist traditions. It is normally repeated when meditating in order to aid focus. You may in fact already have a personal mantra. But I am suggesting that you also have a quasi-mantra: "I am a god". You can say it out loud or just keep repeating it in your head. You can repeat this as often and as long as you like, and sitting in your sacred place and repeating it as you go through the previous practice will definitely enhance the experience and help to recall the fact when you most need to. Set yourself a time (even just 5 or 10 minutes) to carry out this little meditation, and stick to it.

- There are apps that you can acquire on your phone which you can set for a bell to go off at various times during the day. If you have one of these (or even an alarm) it will help you to remember throughout the day.
- Select a totem animal, something that is meaningful to you and something that represents strength to you. It could be a lion or a stallion or a bear. Anything that, when you see it, reminds you not only how powerful you are, but that you are a god. When you have selected your totem, place pictures or sculptures of the animal in various places. And, because we tend not to notice objects when we see them always in the same place, change the locations from time to time.
- You can also have other physical aids: a bracelet or other wrist tie which is meaningful to you; or a ring; or something on your wristwatch that will always remind you.
- When you feel secure about acknowledging that you are a god, you can talk about being a god with your male friends and, especially with your goddess. Find ways to support each other in your god-ness. Talking about it will help an-

THE GOD THAT YOU ARE

chor in your remembering, so be clear that you are creating positive reinforcement not negative reinforcement. You can also have an agreement with your goddess for you to gently remind each other, especially if times become difficult. Not "you're a man, be tough and deal with this!" and definitely not "I would have expected better from you." More along the lines of "I'm reminding you that you are a god, and I believe in you".

- Choose a 'god-name' for yourself. It might be a secret name that only you use, it might be something you share with others. The meaning might be important to you or the sound of the name resonates with something inside you. Whatever, the name should fill you with power and ennoble you.

- Think about the times when you are least likely to remember. Most likely this will be when you are overcome by your emotions, especially if they relate to past experiences. Therefore what you can do is to find some time and a space to be, and write down all the occasions you can think of when you are most likely to forget. Then close your eyes and, one occasion at a time, imagine yourself having that experience (if any of these imaginings bring up unpleasant memories, all the better for this purpose). See yourself in this situation. Then see what happened and how the situation might have had a different outcome if you had remembered that you were a god. Do this with great consciousness and awareness. Then pledge yourself that, if you were ever in the same (or similar) situation again, you would do your best to respond as a god. If your list is long, don't feel that you have to go through the whole list. You can always continue another time. Remember to breathe deeply and slowly throughout this exercise.

It's important to repeat this: If there are occasions where you know that you often get emotionally overwhelmed (in other words, that you're not thinking as clearly as you might), then the very next time one of those occasions occurs stop and pull back slightly. Focus your mind on what is happening. This is your opportunity to break this pattern or habit. Be clear in yourself what has triggered the specific emotion or emotions. Then respond, not solely from that part of you but as an integrated god.

- Another thing that you can do is to have a written reminder in a prominent place. And you can read it out loud to yourself on a regular basis or whenever you need it. This is my own message, (but you can write whatever is meaningful to you):
I call upon all the powers and ask existence to fill my heart with love, to strengthen my core energy, to make me healthy in body, mind and spirit, to heighten my masculinity, to expand my confidence, to allow me the wisdom and clear sight I need to follow my true path

Don't beat yourself up or judge yourself for forgetting that you're a god. After all, you're changing a lifetime's worth of behaviour. And this kind of self-remembering often requires a great deal of application.

George Gurdjieff described 'self-remembering' as a state of consciousness in which human beings are simultaneously aware of both themselves and their actions: "Self-consciousness is the moment when a man is aware both of himself and of his machine. We have it in flashes, but only in flashes. There are moments when you become aware not only of what you are doing but also of yourself doing it. You see both 'I' and the 'here' of 'I am here' – both the anger and the 'I' that is angry. Call this self-remembering, if you like. Now when you are fully and always aware of the 'I' and what it is doing, you become conscious of yourself."

What you're also attempting to do is to respond from your Higher Self, and not react from your baser instincts. In other words, to not be *controlled* by those baser, more primitive instincts.

When you're not used to this practice of self-remembering, it can be very tiring. In which case you sometimes need to give yourself permission to not remember. And, when that happens, you can be okay with that too occasionally. You will find, that, like many things – for example learning to play a musical instrument or learning a new language – with more practise, it becomes easier and less tiring.

Notwithstanding all that I have written above (and all that this book is about) you are, and always will be, a work in progress. Fulfilling your destiny requires time, application, patience and understanding. And, not unlike the ancient Japanese concept of *Wabi-sabi*, you are simultaneously already perfect and can never actually be 'perfect'. What is important is that you always do your best within whatever capabilities you possess. And, remember, you cannot 'fail' in being a god. You are already that.

WHEN OTHERS SAY 'NO, YOU'RE NOT A GOD'

Here is a fundamental truth: You can know something yourself without feeling the need to share that information with others. And, basically, it's nobody else's business what you generally believe in life. You have absolutely no obligation whatsoever to tell anyone anything about yourself (regardless of what *they* say). Whether you know yourself to be a god is not for them to agree with or not agree with. If you are a little unsure of your god-ness it may not be a good idea to share your god-ness with people whom you feel may not understand or who may just want to mock you. This is particularly true if you have boundaries which are susceptible to others' input. Besides, do you really want other people deciding who or what you are? This is for you alone to decide.

So, especially when you're in the early stages of trying to change your behaviour, you might find that you need all the help that you can get. This is why I suggest that you work closely with your beloved or your trusted friends. In this way you can support each other. For the time being do not declare yourself to others. Later, when you are more certain in yourself, you may feel like sharing.

If you are challenged by others about being a god, you could, of course, just say "Read the book". And it is simply enough to tell people "I know the truth about myself".

But you might find that it isn't enough to deter negativity. The best way to do that would be to think through very carefully why you know that you are a god. Put it into words and use those words with people whom you trust. Listen to what they say about how they know that they too are gods, and see if what they say is also true for you.

Ultimately you will be able to tell people that you are a god. If they don't accept it, that's their problem. Above all, don't feel the need to defend yourself or justify to them why or how you are a god.

12: GETTING CLEAR IN YOURSELF AND ABOUT YOURSELF

> **'Look at your life today – at what you're doing, and how you're living your life'**

What do you want in life? You have a limited amount of time in this lifetime. So, how do you want to live your life? What qualities do you desire? What kind of lifestyle suits you? How do you want to relate to other people? Are you a family man, a worker bee, a joiner of associations, a loner, a spiritual man, an enjoyer of creature comforts, a traveller, a sports fan, academically inclined, an eco warrior, a bon vivant, a fitness fanatic, an entertainer?

When you were a small boy you may have wanted to earn your living from a particular job or profession. Possibly, as you grew a little older, you realized that each occupation comes with a particular lifestyle. And, sometimes, we accept a lifestyle even though it's not exactly how we would choose to live if we had a choice. For example, sitting at a desk for eight hours a day.

So here's a question that you could ask yourself: If you won the lottery and didn't have to work for a living, how would you live your life? First of all where would you live?

Secondly, what would you do during the day? What pace of life would you live at? What kind of interactions with other people would you have? What else might you do that you're not currently doing? For example, volunteering with a charity. Would you be more creative? Would you read more? Would you get more exercise? Would you socialize more? Would you travel more? Would you develop your intellect, or your core being, or some skill or ability? What is true for *you*?

Are you currently heading in those directions? Of course, with the mouse-wheel that many men run on today, coupled with their family commitments, they often put these things last (and, often, don't even go close to some of them). And then they reach a certain age, their forties say, or retirement age, and they wonder "what have I done with my life?". So, instead of waiting until it's too late, I suggest that you start asking yourself these questions today. Now! What do you want? What do you need? Exactly how can you live your life so that you and the people around you can be happier?

Going back to that time when you were a small boy: in all likelihood what you wanted to be then was different from what you wanted as you grew up, and is probably different from what you do now. In fact, it's quite likely that what you wanted five years ago is different from what you might want today. We change all the time. Our bodies change. Our minds change. We have new experiences. We drop some fears and get more confidence. We become more aware of various possibilities and, (hopefully) we become more edified.

Look at your life today – at what you're doing and how you're living your life. This may well be what you wanted five (or even two) years ago. But is it what you want *now*? Then project yourself into the future. Make a five-year plan and a ten-year plan. Be very detailed. Keep the 'good' aspects of your life and figure out a way to deal with the rest.

Is there something you're doing right now or some way that you're living your life that you're not happy with? Can you drop it? If so, then drop it! Right now. No 'ifs' no 'buts' no excuses. Drop it.

There's something else to think about too. And, in fact, you might have already been considering this. The world is changing faster and faster. Occupations that have existed in the past no longer exist. There's even less call for seemingly always-necessary jobs. What are you doing at the moment? If you're a doctor you're probably always going to be needed (although there's no absolute guarantee about even that). However, if you're, say, a newspaper printer you've probably already thought a lot about the future. How do you believe your occupation is going to fare in five or ten years?

So it might be time to revue your career anyway. And, while you're doing that, consider *how* you want to live your life.

Of course there's more to your life than how you earn a living. And, indeed, how you occupy your leisure time. What kind of a man do you actually want to be? Just getting along? Mediocre? Average? Managing OK? Happy with what you've done and think that's enough? Well, good luck to you. And I really mean that. If you truly believe in your heart that's all you need in life to make you happy and that, on the day you die you'll look back satisfied with that, then I wish you the very best of luck and have a happy life.

On the other hand if you think you're going to look back with regrets on the day you die, then now is the time to do something about that. Now!

You may, of course, already have an inkling of some regrets. But I'm not so much talking about what you've done in your life, but what you *haven't* yet done.

It's fashionable these days for people to compile bucket lists. These might involve, say, travel or jumping out of airplanes, or bungee jumping. I believe compiling a bucket list to be a valid exercise. As I said, I'm sure that when you die you'd like to have as few regrets as possible.

But we're concerned now with *be*ing rather than *do*ing. What kind of a man would you like to *be*? You might consider writing a list of all the qualities that you respect and admire in men. Think of men that you've known. What was it about them that shone through to you? Maybe there was a genuineness about them, maybe they were heroes in some way, maybe they were 'successful'. Be careful here not to compare yourself unfavourably with other men. If, for example, you admire a man because he was successful in business and you feel that you could never emulate that success, then that would not be helpful to you. But, if you look at what it was about the man that made him successful, you might find qualities in him that you *can* emulate.

What is it about yourself that you like right now? Would you say, for example, that you're reliable, trustworthy, a good friend? If not, why not? Are you sincere, honourable, passionate, empathetic, considerate, a loving man? If not, why not? Do you care about your community? Are you fair and honest in all your dealings? Are you faithful? Are you loyal? These are all qualities that you can develop in yourself without anybody else's input, without money, and without the need for 'good luck'.

I'm sure that you could find many additional qualities relating to the way that you could be which would enhance your self-respect.

There have been countless discussions about whether we have a purpose in life. What do you believe? Perhaps you belong to an organized religion that already espouses what your purpose in life might be. Perhaps you've already philosophized about the subject in detail.

There are a variety of possible responses to the question "Is there a purpose to being here?". Many people hold strong beliefs. There are some who believe that, in fact, there is no purpose in life. 'We're here because we're here' might be their dictum.

I happen to believe that mankind does have a purpose in life. As I mentioned earlier, I believe that our purpose is to advance ourselves as far as we can go. And the way that we do that is by individuals developing *them*selves. In other words, it is our obligation to humanity to be the best that we can possibly be.

But what is it that gives us a sense of purpose, so that, rather than just drifting through life, we are imbued with that sense. What gives *you* a sense of purpose? What inspires you? What engages you and makes you feel good – especially lasting feelings of satisfaction, joy, pleasure, contentment, pride and elation? How often do you engage with activities that bring about these feelings? Could you do them more often?

How often do you set yourself an intention and then strive to achieve it? What do you aim for? Robert Browning in his poem *Andrea del Sarto* wrote "…a man's reach should exceed his grasp, or what's a heaven for?…". The point of this is that you might gain satisfaction from easily and successfully achieving an outcome. But when the task at hand is more difficult, a successful outcome can be even more rewarding. So you can increase your sense of purpose by sometimes aiming higher. If you succeed it will give you a much greater level of satisfaction. If you don't succeed as highly as you'd like, keep going or find an alternative aim. There's no shame in acknowledging a gap between aspiration and outcome. There is no 'failure'. All that happens is that your understanding of the outcome doesn't match your expectation. But what matters is not really whether you succeed or fail. It's that you do your best. And, by 'best', I mean that you apply yourself .to the maximum of your ability.

It happens in life that we sometimes don't have any ambitions. If that happens to you, the first question that you might ask yourself is what is important to *you*. Not what is important to your mother, your beloved, your church, but *you*. What floats your boat? What gets your juices flowing? What makes you want to get out of bed in the morning? Is it the thought of some activity or interaction with others? Is it creating something, not just objects, but music, writing, ideas,

What captures your imagination? Where do you find your thoughts straying to? What do you want to have conversations about with other people? (Note, I'm not saying 'What are you currently talking about', but what do you *want* to have conversations with other people about?) What subjects do you like to read about? When do you feel yourself come alive?

Answering these questions will help you find the area that you're interested in. Maybe there are several areas. In which case, compile a list, prioritising your level of passion and interest from the top to te bottom.

Once you've discovered the area(s) that you're interested in, your next step is to discover how that subject relates to you and which aspect of it most interests you. Then you need to answer a question: Are you generally an active person or a passive person? For example are you more likely to start an association or join an existing one? Or, in fact, are you not interested in being part of an association? I'm not suggesting that you should be interested in any associations. This is merely a way to discover whether you're more active or passive. Because it may be that you need other people to help you to discover your passion. If this is in fact the case, then I suggest you talk with your friends and associates and ask them what their passions are. You might not share their passion, but it will give you some clues.

Forget for the moment whether you're competent to do anything in the area of your interest(s). Forget whether you actually currently do anything. You have just gone through an important process of discovering something about yourself.

You might rack your brain and not be able to think of a single thing that you'd like to do, that interests you, or a way you'd like to be. You might just feel awash in a sea of indecision or disinterest. If you have gone through all these processes and this is your outcome, then I suggest that you don't criticize yourself for that. Maybe this is the wrong time in your life to be searching. On the other hand, this might be the story of your life. And, you might just not actually have any ambitions. You may be quite content to take each second as it comes and live life in the moment. This might make you happy, and you can't see why it wouldn't make you happy in the future.

If this is your truth, then that's great. I encourage you to live your life that way and not worry about having to have ambitions, aims or even desires. Perhaps living this way actually is your vocation and your purpose. Again, you can become aware of something about yourself.

What is important here, however, is knowing as much about yourself as possible so that you can function to your absolute optimum. It also goes to discovering what you are capable of. You may wish to push or stretch your boundaries by attempting tasks about which you may be doubtful of your 'success'. You could try different things in different areas. And remember Robert Burns' spider: "If at first you don't succeed - try, try again". Just call it Version 1.0 and move on to Version 2.0.

Many men underestimate their abilities. And they either don't start or they quit easily. Giving up before you give yourself a chance is the only 'failure'. Think about some highly complex world for a moment. You might instantly say "Oh, I couldn't possibly do that". And I'm not suggesting that you jump into doing brain surgery in your kitchen! But, with the proper training and facilities, I'd hazard a guess that you wouldn't be as inept at many things as you might think.

Don't underestimate yourself and what you're capable of.

In order to find out more about yourself, get out into the world as much as you can. Not to compare yourself with others, but to edify yourself. Make your life richer. Read more – both fact and fiction. And while you're reading, absorb as much as you can, not just about the different cultures, but about the lives of others – how they live, why they do what they do. The same is true of films, whether factual or fiction. Broaden your understanding of how other people exist. Try to see their motivations, what drives them, what their hopes, dreams and desires are. Contrast them with your own. Not to see whether either is superior, but just a simple assessment. Look at how other people deal with situations, especially similar situations to those in which you might find yourself. Look at their triggers. How do they respond (or react)? Does this offer a choice for you?

Travel more, both within your own country and overseas. Expose yourself to other cultures, especially cultures where there are different ways of doing things. Look, listen and feel the similarities and the differences. Again, without judgment, evaluate your life and those around you: their moralities, mores, and priorities might be totally different to your own. Open yourself up to understanding how life is for them. And, for those who need reminding, travel is more than about finding exotic bars to get drunk in and unthinkingly taking photographs and posting them on social media. Just being in a 'foreign' environment can have an impact on you. And it can also assist in your development. For example, if you are an impatient man, try going to a country like India where your impatience will cause you to tear your hair out. Just being in that country and having to deal with things the way people in India do will help to teach you patience and help to teach you to surrender.

Have conversations with others that go deeper than talking about sport, politics, the weather or the latest fad. Both the traditional media and social media seem to be fixated on war and disasters, often presenting highly simplistic black and white views. But it's in the grey areas that it becomes interesting. There's always more than one perspective on any subject. It's possible to look at the various shades of grey and try to understand what is really going on. And you don't have to have a degree in philosophy to do this. Neither do you need to be attached to any one particular viewpoint. Try playing the devil's advocate occasionally (I suggest that you tell your friends that this is what you're doing). It will help you to understand more about the subject. Discussing more esoteric subjects can also be enlightening. Remember, you don't have to have a pre-existing viewpoint on any subject. This can be a dialogue where you explore subjects together. You could go even further and research your subject matter to discover new details, and then share the results with your friends.

There is an ancient parable from the Indian subcontinent. It goes something like this: Five blind men are travelling together across the country. They come across an unknown creature which is an elephant, but which none of them instantly recognizes. Each of the men touches a different part of the animal. The first man who feels the trunk says the creature obviously is like the branch of a tree. The next man, who feels a leg says no, the elephant is like a pillar. The third blind man reaches up and feels a tusk. He says the elephant is actually like a solid pipe. The man who feels the tail says the elephant is definitely like a rope. At which the last man feels an ear. He says "You're all wrong. This creature is shaped like a kind of fan. Each of the men is convinced that he is right and the others are wrong. (The point of the parable is obviously that all things are subjective and frequently depend upon your perspective.)

But how much better it might have been if each of the men invited all the others to also touch the part he had touched. Then there might have been some genuine empathy and real sharing.

Travel does that too. It shows you how other people live their lives and it offers you their perspective on life.

And, in your own country, talk to people from other cultures too. Let them tell you what their beliefs are without needing to respond, let alone argue with them. Then share your own beliefs and understandings without needing for them to agree or be swayed by what you say. If you receive an invitation to go to their home, go. If you receive an invitation to go to their place of worship, even if you don't believe in organized religion or you're firmly established in your own beliefs, take up the offer. The same applies to functions like weddings. You can learn something from all of these experiences. And they will all broaden your mind and enrich you.

And, while we're at it, listen to what women say about what it is like living as a woman. Do this with a completely open heart and open mind, without any judgment. Don't take anything personally that a woman may tell you: she's simply talking about herself. You may learn a great deal: about women, about relationships, and about life.

As you receive input from all of these sources see the information and experiences as ways of developing yourself. How could you improve the quality of your life? How could you evolve as a man? Which of these details will enhance your character and build you into a solid being? Sift through what you learn. You don't have to take anything on, but there are bound to be valuable advantages to be gained from going through this process.

How would you describe yourself right now? If you had to write a few paragraphs about your character what would you say. For example, would you say that you're upstanding, introverted, extroverted, brave, ordinary, lovable, honest, reliable, unreliable, prejudiced, lazy, hard-working, or entrepreneurial. What words would you use?

How do you think other people would describe you? Try and see yourself through others' eyes. What words might they use?

Or try and see yourself as someone else. How would you describe that person?

When you've had the chance to really think all of this through, ask yourself whether you're happy with the answers that you come up with. Are there areas where you feel that you could grow? Are there things about yourself that you'd like to change? If there are, CHANGE THEM. Don't wait until tomorrow. Do it now. There's only one person who can do this. And there's not a second to waste.

13: IMPROVING YOUR SKILL SET

> **'A god is a multifaceted and a fully-rounded being'**

This subject normally comes up with regard to employment because often the more skills you have, the more employable you are.

However, that's not the main reason why I'm talking about it here. The reason is because a god is multifaceted and a fully-rounded being. He may not be an expert in everything, but he is au fait with a great many things. He does not restrict himself to one or two areas of life, but finds interest in, and attempts, a wide variety of activities. Each time you challenge yourself in a new area you will grow. And each time you master a task you will grow even more.

In learning a new skill or attempting a new task you will stretch yourself. And, as you stretch, so you will grow. This is indispensable, because development and growth are essentials in being a god.

Being a more fully-rounded and multifaceted being is not only desirable in itself, but will make you a more interesting (and therefore more attractive) man. And this, in turn, will sustain and nurture you.

In the past it was considered usual that a man was only capable of one occupation. And men often stuck to one job their whole life. Also in those days one might hear the expression "Jack of all trades, master of none", which was a derisive comment.

However, that situation has changed dramatically. Modern technology has opened up a vast number of opportunities for exploration. The number of potential occupations has increased exponentially and it is not considered abnormal to change jobs – and even complete careers – almost on a regular basis. In fact it is now considered that you will have an advantage if you bring a wider level of experience to any future position.

These days there are also a much greater number of possible non-money-making, activities. And, here too, modern technology has offered men more opportunities to express themselves. The vast 'big box' hardware palaces are thriving with men tackling all sorts of enterprises. There are also numerous shops that sell all kinds of materials with which to express your creativity. These go way beyond hobbies and 'little jobs around the house'. Now it's possible for a man to be as creative as his imagination will allow.

Probably the greatest wonder of the modern age has been the internet. Here you can not only discover information about just about any subject, but you can find assistance in learning to do or play something. In fact there are, in reality, far too many possibilities and one has to be practical about time and energy considerations. Nevertheless it's all there for you take advantage of.

Again, it's not just about *making* something – or even *doing* something. Developing your skill set is also about *being*. It's about *who* you are and your desire to fully embrace all your possibilities. It's about being open and not limiting yourself, because limitation is a kind of living death. It's also about attitude. *Your* attitude. If you possess a 'can-do' or 'have-a-go' attitude in your skill development, that will have a knock-on effect with regard to the rest of your life.

All of these new opportunities also allow you to think of yourself differently. I sometimes run creativity workshops. One of the questions I ask at the beginning of the workshop is "Do you consider yourself to be a creative person". At least half the participants will often say "no". However, during the course of the workshop, many participants realize that they have a depth of creativity that they rarely allow. This is often because they have been told that they're not creative, and so they never even try. I remember one man who said that he wasn't a creative person. And yet, once we started talking, he told us that he was an inventor. What could be more creative than that!

It helps, of course to select areas that are of most interest to you. But, occasionally, a good challenge would be to develop a part of life that you might not ordinarily be drawn to.

Consider what actors do. A good actor will not simply act a role – he is not pretending to be another person, he becomes the man that he is playing. He inhabits that man and who he is. He is not simply giving a shallow portrait of the man's persona.

Of course it's not given to us all to be great actors or even good, professional actors. However, in terms of expanding your skill set and developing yourself, you might consider trying out temporarily being something that you're not. For example, if you're by nature an introverted man, one time *be* an extrovert. Be extrovert as though you were an actor. Think of it as a role that you're playing. Express yourself, talk loudly, laugh out loud, or wear strange clothing. There are several opportunities to do this without alarming your friends too much. There are clown schools and other workshops. There are fancy dress parties. Some offices even have 'Talk like a Pirate' days. Or you could just get together with your friends and agree that this is what you're all going to do. And, in the midst of being extrovert, check in with yourself. How does this feel? Are there areas of discomfort that you might want to explore later? Does part of you revel in being like this. Would this part of you like to be alive more often?

Another way to increase your expansion is to try to feel what it might be like to belong to a culture other than the one in which you were brought up. Of course, to some extent, this 'feeling' is only going to be in your imagination. But you can bolster the reality of it by talking with people from other cultures, reading about them, watching films, going to museums, and even walking around parts of your town that you might not ordinarily visit. Go into shops and see for yourself what's on offer. If there are strange foodstuffs look up recipes that contain these ingredients. You could even host a dinner to celebrate this culture. The idea, of course, is not to mock or appropriate this culture, but to celebrate it and to explore a different part of you. You won't become instantly, say, Indian or African. But you will enhance parts of yourself which don't often get exercised, and this will contribute to your overall growth.

As I said earlier, ask your Beloved and other women what it's like to be a woman. Just listen and take in what they say. This is not an opportunity for you to comment, it's an opportunity for you to learn. Take careful note of what they say. This information will stand you in good stead for the rest of your life. Widening your knowledge of what it's like being a woman will, again, contribute to your overall growth. In addition it will also enable you to better empathize, help you in your relationships generally with women and, specifically, deepen your romantic relationships.

Active listening

If you are having an intellectual conversation with someone where they are telling you about their thoughts and beliefs, that's one thing. I hope that you would listen to them with an open mind and consider their perspective before answering. And, after that, you may want to express your opinion.

However, if somebody tells you something that they feel (even if it sounds like a 'thought' to you) or something about themselves, do not immediately rebut it. After all, they are sharing something with you about *them*. Listen with an open heart. Be sure to take it in and try and understand what they are telling you. This is not an opportunity for you to 'agree' or 'disagree' with them. Because, for many people, if it sounds like you're rejecting their 'argument' (in fact, their feeling), then it feels to them as though you are rejecting *them*. This is your chance to gain greater insight, and therefore expand your wisdom.

14: HEALING YOURSELF

> **'What happened to you? What were the impacts that made you who you are today?'**

Much like any growing thing, from the very beginning we are affected by our environment and the way in which we are treated. If you plant a tree in rich soil and water it and feed it and care for it, the tree will probably grow strong and healthy. However, if it is planted in a situation which is inhospitable – for example the wrong type of soil – and it is not nurtured properly, or it is exposed to extreme wind and rain or is physically damaged in some way, it will either not grow healthily or it will develop abnormal characteristics.

And so it is with human beings – right from the beginning. If you were not breast-fed at all that is going to have an effect on you. If you were not given appropriate nutritional care or medical attention when you needed it that too is going to affect you. If you were not given enough affection or nurture, that is also going to affect you. If you were physically or sexually abused as a child you are bound to have a major reaction to that and you will have to find some way to deal with that if you are to survive.

There are so many things which impact on us as we are growing and developing, and not all of them are obvious. If you have siblings, then your position (and role) in the family will often cause you to behave in a particular way. If you only had one parent, or your parents separated when you were young, you would have found a way to cope with that. If you were part of a large family and/or greater family then that too will have an effect on you.

On a tree it is often possible to see the various traumas that have occurred during its lifetime. You can see all the gnarly bits and all the twists and turns. But, with a human being, the traumas are more hidden. Sometimes you can see it in somebody's facial expressions or body language. Sometimes you can see it in their behaviour. Sometimes their lifestyle 'choices' reflect their upbringing and what happened to them during childhood and adolescence.

The question is what happened to you? What were the impacts – major and minor – that made you who you are today? And, let's be clear, I'm not just talking about negative impacts. Hopefully there was also input in your life which had positive consequences, and it's good to also see where things are working for you.

It is fashionable these days to talk about 'healing'. And the healing that this often refers to is not just healing of the body, but healing of the spirit, healing of the psyche, and emotional healing. All this is done so that we can function in the way that we were designed to function.

If you are angry all the time there's a reason for that. If your self-esteem is poor there's a reason for that. If you always have difficulties with relationships, or there is frequent sadness, or you have certain compulsions or obsessions or addictions, there's a reason for that.

So that's why it's important to understand why you do what you do. Because if you're still *reacting* from a childhood trauma, then ultimately it might be very difficult to fully inhabit yourself. And you need to heal the trauma as best you can so that you can perform with full integrity.

In many cases it is extremely valuable to work with a professional therapist who works in this area. The best therapists don't tell you what's wrong with you, but help you discover for yourself in which areas you need to 'work'.

A good therapist will help your psyche heal in the same way that a good physician will help your body to heal: they will work with you in searching out the cause; they will offer various remedies; and they will support you while you go through the process and healing is brought about.

In addition to one-on-one counselling there are also a huge number of organisations offering workshops or groups of various kinds. These come in many guises. They can be very useful and can provide you with great insight into where you might need healing. I have personally had some major breakthroughs in my own life working in this way.

HOWEVER, I suggest that you check the bona fides of the actual people running the courses in these organisations very carefully before you open yourself up to them. Just being 'trained' by an organisation is not good enough. Remember that these people hold your mental health and wellbeing in their hands. I have known of several cases of people who came out with more problems than they went in with. There can be 'side-effects' in group therapy just as there can be with medications for the body. The facilitators should ideally at least have some form of psychological care training (not just a '1-week Intensive Training') and preferably they should be properly qualified.

You can also talk with people who have previously participated. But if you do, I suggest that their participation occurred some time prior to the time of your discussion. A neophyte, still glowing after a recent workshop may not be your best reference. They should have had some life experience since they participated, to see (and be able to share with you) how the workshop helped them in their life.

Writing is an excellent way to reveal any traumas or incidents in your earlier life that might now be causing you not to function optimally. And here I'm not just talking about your childhood. It is possible to be traumatised at any age. Relationships, in particular, can bring about many unwanted tendencies. Writing about your life can be very cathartic too, in that, when you reveal an episode to yourself and examine it in 'broad daylight', you will be in a position to release any trauma that may have occurred.

You may, of course, have suffered *severe* trauma in certain areas and you may not only be highly aware of these events, but *painfully* aware. However, the type of traumas that I'm talking about are of the hidden or less obvious kind; ones which you have to trawl through your memory to rediscover.

One way to do this is to start at the very beginning. Use old photographs or other material and, starting with your earliest days, collate them together with written descriptions about your life at that time and incidents in your life. For example, you could write about when you were three years old. (You might find a picture of yourself at that age.) You might remember that you had an uncle who used to visit often. He may have bounced you up and down on his lap and, just for a laugh, he might have let you drop onto the floor. Write about those times. How did you feel as a 3-year old? What were the emotions that came up, and how has it affected your relationships with older men (especially bigger men)? This is just an example. You will have thousands of memories that you can dredge up and write about. By no means all of them will have been traumatic. And, hopefully, a great many of them will be happy memories. But some might have been traumatic. And some of them might be directly affecting you today.

Progress chronologically through your life. For each incident try and feel what you took away from the experience. Was there a determination to behave differently? Did the experience crimp your life in some way? Did you change direction as a direct result? And are you happy about that direction?

Were there moments in your life when something happened to you that others (your father or mother a sibling or teacher or scoutmaster) described as "character-building"? If so, think very carefully about those times. Can you remember how you felt at the time? Has that feeling stayed with you? Do you agree that what happened was, in fact, beneficial to you?

If you can see these moments in your life for what they were and if you can see that they impacted on your life in a negative way, you will now be in a better position, if you choose, to reverse the situation by examining what the take-away message was and by turning that around so that you can now give yourself a positive message.

This is also the time to look at all the ways in which you are self-sabotaging today and to stop that process. Can you be clear with yourself how you either prevent yourself from pursuing a positive direction or allow yourself to follow negative activities? Can you look 'behind the scenes' to see why you do that, and what secondary gain you receive from doing that? Can you see any fears that come up about what might happen if you were to pursue a positive direction? Once you've brought all this into your conscious mind it is now time to address it. Make a decision. Face those fears and move along your correct destiny path. Allow those doubts and fears to fall away because they are not serving you well and are hindering your healing.

As part of your healing process and, in order to be as complete as possible, it's also time to heal your relationships. (And I'm not just referring to romantic relationships.) If there is someone in your life (or, in fact more than one person) with whom your relationship is fraught, now is the time also to either let go of the relationship or to at least get clear in yourself about the relationship, especially if it's a particularly toxic one.

Can you see whether at least some of your energy is locked up by fraught relationships? If you could access and release that locked-up energy you could not only do more with your life, but *be* more. You would be more integrated as a god and your overall energy would be less adulterated.

If you have difficulties in relating then, presumably, you've already tried to resolve matters between you and others and, if apologies are appropriate, you've done that, even if you believe that something wasn't your 'fault'. (If you haven't done that, then do it *immediately*). Forget your own feelings and any hurts involved for a moment and try to put yourself in the position of others. What motivates them? Why are they unhappy? What expectations do they have? Once you've seen these things you can accept that there are (at least) two sides to every story. And you can accept that sometimes people just can't agree and can't 'sort things out'. Perhaps this is an on-going situation where there's a difference of opinion or simply a clash of personalities. I'm not talking about forgiveness. This is acceptance. It's life. Get over it. Carrying this energy is not serving *you*. Move on.

Sometimes, in the case of family or work relationships, it's impossible to drop the relationships altogether. And, sometimes, for whatever reason, it is not possible to discuss the situation, either because you feel that it's inappropriate (in work situations, say) or because as soon as you try to talk about these matters it seems to inflame the other. In which case I suggest that you find a neutral person such as a therapist with whom you can unload your feelings (without expectations that they will say you're "right"). Get clear that your relationship with this person is detrimental to your wellbeing and have minimal contact with them. BUT, make sure that you don't become passive/aggressive. In other words, respond to their communications with humanity (without ever feeling that you have to justify yourself). Keep conversations brief but polite. It's not up to you to initiate communication or work towards maintaining a relationship.

Remember that what we're talking about here is healing yourself, so the best thing that you can do in these situations is to focus your attention on other relationships and other areas of your life.

Perspective can play a big role in healing. If you are able to take time out by yourself, preferably in a place where you don't usually go, you will find it easier to get clearer about yourself. Look deeply into yourself. What needs to be resolved inside you? What's not working as well as you'd like? In which ways are you not integrated? Being integrated is like being able to unlock a door and step through into a beautiful, clear existence. And the tumblers of the lock are your mind, body, and emotions, If these are not in alignment then the lock will not work smoothly and will not open. In which case you cannot step through. And it is the ability to step through that we are fundamentally talking about.

So that's why it's important that each of these elements is working optimally and why you need to work on and heal them simultaneously. All three areas are closely connected and, for example, healing your psyche will have a positive impact on both your emotional life and your physical life.

As you heal you can let go of those things that required healing. However, sometimes we forget that we've healed and we revert to old patterns. This is easy to do and very common, especially if those patterns are deeply ingrained. The ego, too, sometimes has an investment in you not changing your ways.

I suggest that, as you proceed, you make a note of those areas which you've worked on healing, so that, from time to time, you can refer to your notes and remind yourself. I further suggest that you write them 'old-school', that is, by hand on paper. There are a couple of reasons for this. Firstly, the physical act of writing will actually reinforce those details in your brain and help you to remember more successfully what you have put behind you. Secondly, a piece of paper (or a book) as a physical object is much harder to ignore than a file on your phone or your computer (especially if you put the paper or book in a prominent place). I also suggest that you make a habit of referring to these written notes. This way you will also be able to see your progress.

15: FINDING YOUR CENTRE AGAIN IF YOU LOSE IT

> **'It's important to be as centred as possible for as long as possible'**

What does it mean to you to be 'centred' in yourself? Well, this is what it means to be *un*-centred: You do not focus on events properly; you make poor judgment calls; you have accidents; you overreact to comments and other triggers; your awareness and consciousness levels drop; you're running only on a limited number of cylinders; your memory will degrade; you will have imperfect control over your body and worse hand-eye coordination. And each of these things will impact on the others.

So that's why it's important to be as centred as possible for as long as possible; at the very least so that you can function to your optimum simply as a man. But, here, we're talking about not just being a man, but actually being a god. And, therefore, it's even more imperative that you remain in your centre.

In terms of techniques as to how to do that, the first 'technique' is to realize when you're *not* centred. This can actually be harder than it seems. When we're fired up about something in the heat of the moment, or we're anxious, or we're time-stressed, it's very easy to not only lose our centre, but be unaware that we've done that. Therefore, the ability to notice this is fundamental to our wellbeing. That's why the awareness and consciousness that we talked about earlier are crucial to remaining centred.

The next 'technique' is to metaphorically take a 'step back' from where you are. Once you have become aware that you're not as balanced or centred as you could be, pause. Reflect on the moment and acknowledge your lack of being centred.

Then: breathe. Long, slow and deep. Close your eyes and breathe into your belly and allow both the inhalations and exhalations to be as long as possible. Breathe until you can see everything as though it's all in slow motion.

The ideal is to act immaculately at all times, but that is the <u>ideal</u>. Don't castigate yourself if you can't do this all the time. Just try and remember as best you can at all times.

And don't begin apportioning blame, either to yourself or others. Blaming is a distraction that serves no purpose. By all means accept responsibility for something if you need to. But that's all. It happened, now it's time to move on.

Remember your sense of humour. It often really helps to be able to laugh in many circumstances. Not only will the laughter take the heat out of a situation, but it can also radically change how you feel about something. For example, maybe you were making something more 'important' than it really is. Laughter also has the added benefit of helping you to breathe better and to relax your body.

Now you know that you can improve how you are. What else is needed at this point? Do you need to think more slowly and more clearly? Do you need to block out extraneous sounds and vision?

Do you need to be by yourself? Do you need to stretch your body and move around to shift your energy?

Come back into yourself. Remember that you're a god. Feel your god-power flowing through you. You are the master of yourself. You've got this handled.

When you have re-centred yourself it's time to gain some perspective. There are some things that you need to do: Firstly, discover what it was that un-centred you. What were the events leading up to the time you found yourself to be un-centred? Were you distracted by something outside of you, or were you perhaps distracted by your own thoughts? Were you feeling tired? Was there something happening in your body? What emotions were you feeling at the time? Next, what lesson can you learn from this experience? Is there something about it that would help you to be more centred in the future?

When you're walking around feel the power of the earth and connect with that. When you're in a social situation don't make yourself separate from others, but be aware of your own god-ness. And recognize that god-ness in others when you see it.

Thoroughness might be something different for everyone. In terms of application and precision, that is. The word 'thorough' means "performed with or showing great care and completeness". That is, 'complete' with regard to every detail. For some men 'close enough is good enough'. Their thoroughness might not be your thoroughness. And, indeed, it might not be the same as someone with OCD (unless you do actually have OCD!). So your level of thoroughness is very subjective. Nevertheless, I encourage you to take the greatest care that you can.

Sometimes, however, it's tempting to not complete things properly or do a slapdash job. And this either comes because we're rushed for time, or we don't care enough about the job in hand.

Or because we're not centred properly. Preparation is a very useful key to thoroughness:
- Thinking something through before you begin;
- Planning your course of events and the various stages;
- Visualizing a balanced, thorough outcome;
- Having the right situation and tools for the job;
- Having a relaxed body and mind.

In fact this applies not only to a physical 'job', but any activity. For example, making a speech, a hike in the country, or even a meditation session.

If you attempt any activity and find that you're not centred, pause. Reflect on how un-centred you might be. Wait for your energy to catch up and feel your god-ness rising up through your body. Be comfortable in your body and feel each part of it; even move your body around so that you feel in full contact with each part of it. Feel the air against your skin. Listen to all the sounds around you and see yourself in situ. Be *present* in this place. Check that your breathing is relaxed and unrestricted. Remember your plan and focus on the details and their order. Visualize carrying out this activity successfully. Act.

There are also times when you don't feel like a Big, Strong Man. Sometimes you might feel like a small boy. My advice is to welcome this. Look at the small children that you know, and see the godliness in them. There is a pure beauty which shines through them. Allow yourself to be vulnerable. Feel the power of that, and let go into it. If you don't feel safe to explore that with other people, then simply be by yourself and feel it. Don't judge it. You are still a god. In fact this is the perfect you.

16: TEACH YOUR SONS TO BE GODS

> **'Your son's edification is in your hands. It is your duty to fulfil that role to your utmost'**

Crosby Stills & Nash sang "Teach your children well". If you have sons, it's never too soon to teach them to be gods also. In fact, the earlier you start to teach them the better. (You can teach your daughters to be goddesses too, but in this book we're focusing on men.)

Your son's edification is in your hands, it is your duty to fulfil that role to your utmost. And that includes encouraging him also to be a god.

Never preach to your son. By that I mean that when you are talking to him be your authentic self and also respect him as an individual. He has as many rights as you do. You will have more knowledge and wisdom and more experience than him, but that's all. You are responsible in law for him and, because you love him, you will want to protect him. But nothing gives you the right to treat him with disrespect. Ever! And there is no need to be heavy with him. Also be aware of nagging him. You probably know what that feels like! Find a balance between instructing him and going over the same ground ad nauseam.

Being a god is the right of every man. Teach your son by example and also talk to him about what it means to be a god. Teach him the difference between "God" and "being a god". That being a god is ultimately about evolving as a man, and also evolving as a human being. It's also about being fully alive. And that includes all challenges and all possibilities. The more that your son can inhabit his godliness the more able he will be to face those challenges and to pursue those possibilities.

Of course, teach him that this is not about being superior to other boys (or men, eventually). It's about being the best that *he* can possibly be. Just as he can improve academically or in any sport or playing any instrument, so too can he improve *himself*. And, as he naturally grows – physically and mentally – he can also grow into his godliness.

Teach him that a big part of knowing who he is means knowing where his boundaries are. Explain the difference between being assertive and being aggressive. And show him that being able to assert his boundaries (without being aggressive) will not only make him more confident and assist with all his relationships, it will also make him more successful as a man, as a human being, and as a god.

Teach him about the qualities of a god: how to maintain his integrity and honour, his dignity and his compassion; how to be love and how to practise love; and how to be aware and conscious. Let him know the difference between being 'graceful' (in the feminine way) and 'living in grace'; that a god is a man who lives in grace, and that 'grace' is not simply a Christian (or *any* religious) belief, but a state that is open to all beings as a way to be.

Also let your son be aware of his ego, that the ego is not to be feared or scorned, but neither is it there to control him, and that he needs to be aware when he is reacting from his ego. And show him what it is like when a man responds with awareness, rather than without awareness and reacting to triggers.

Show him how to heighten his senses so that he can be more aware. Teach him the techniques that you have learned. And allow him to develop his sixth sense, and that men can have intuition and needn't be afraid of it, disparage or dismiss it; that intuition is something to be proud of.

Teach your son the value of being authentic, being real, and being an individual. Show him the value of being flexible, but not following the herd or submitting to peer pressure, and to stand up for what he believes to be right; to be his own man and to be true to himself. Help him to discover and know who he is, what he wants in life, and what his values are. Show him how to prioritise and determine what is most important to him in life.

Discuss with your son what his Higher Self is, and explain the difference between being an ordinary man and a god. And why it is important to achieve his highest potential.

Together with your son explore what it means to be competitive. That, ultimately, it's not about being 'better' than other boys, but about challenging himself.

Teach your son to be proud of his body, to fully inhabit it, and how to care for it. That the better he looks after his body, the more it will reward him later in life. Help him to learn about healthy living in all of its aspects. Especially educate him about developing his mind, not just acquiring knowledge, but also using and exercising his mind.

Talk about stress, how it occurs and how to manage it. Show him what you do to manage your own stress and share your practices with him. Also talk about the value of stress, that it can sometimes be valuable in terms of motivating him, but that he needs to be very clear about how that happens and, in particular, when stress can degrade the quality of his life.

Importantly, talk about emotions, what they are and the role they play in his life. Let him know that, unlike many men who ignore their emotions, a god embraces *all* of his emotions. Show him the connection between thoughts, emotions and actions, and that his emotions play a valuable role in his life.

Share your own past experiences in life with your son. Tell him about how your experiences affected you at the time and what emotions were brought up. Also whether there have been long-term effects on you. Speak from your wisdom.

Your son will be full of potential in a great many areas. And it's never too soon (or too late) for your son to begin discovering what his potential is. By all means make suggestions about what he might want to explore, and encourage him in all areas. Open his eyes to possibilities. But never push him into something with which he doesn't feel comfortable. Find a way to be honest with him about his potentialities, but NEVER put him down. Remember, he can always improve his abilities in any area. Your job is to support and encourage him while he explores possibilities and finds out what is important to him. A great sculptor doesn't insist on imposing his vision on his raw material. He finds the image from his material and allows it to come to him. (Michaelangelo is supposed to have said that, as a sculptor, every block of stone has a figure in it and that it was his task to "liberate that figure from the stone"). Your task is to help your son sculpt himself.

Your son will have some specific gifts, some abilities that come naturally to him. Help him find out what they are. Support him in developing them as *he* develops.

There has been a fashion in recent years for 'helicopter parents' to whisk their children from one extracurricular activity to another. Beware of loading up your son with *your* desires. Keep a close eye on him to make sure that he is not overloaded, and also that he has enough time to do 'nothing'. Also allow him to find and make his own activities.

Most children are born open-minded and open-hearted. It seems that, as they grow older they learn to close up. Encourage your son to remain both open in his mind and open in his heart. Don't fill him up with prejudices, cant, or dogma. With your guidance he can find things out for himself. Steer him clear of negativity, especially about his abilities.

At the same time that you teach him to be *open*-minded also show him what it means to be *strong*-minded. This does not mean being stubborn and willful. It certainly doesn't mean never listening to others. What it means is to take in as much information as possible, then consider the objective facts. And, on that basis, to make up his own mind. I realize that some men might find this difficult. But I'm not suggesting that you're saying "Don't listen to me at all". I'm suggesting that you say "Listen to what I have to offer. Also listen to other perspectives. And then (taking into account his age and relative inexperience) make up his own mind and make his own decisions.

Show him how to love unconditionally. (Actually, he can probably teach you how to do this — because that's what children do. More especially, encourage him to *keep* loving unconditionally.)

Teach your son about the difference between good habits and bad habits. Encourage his good habits and gently discourage any bad habits that he might have. Show him the value of *self*-discipline,

Support him in finding inspiration from many sources; from other men *and* women, as well as other children. But, not only from individual people, but also animals and the environment; and accomplishments from everywhere, regardless of country or culture.

One of the greatest gifts that you can give to your son is to teach him how to accept himself. Of course that starts with you showing him that *you* accept *him*, that you don't judge him, that he is 'good enough'. If you ever feel the need to criticize him, make sure that your criticism is always constructive, so that he knows that you're encouraging him to do and to be his best. Tell him often that you believe in him and you trust him.

Talk to him also about how you accept *your*self. And that this comes about through knowing yourself and understanding yourself. So that the more he knows and understands himself, the more he can accept himself. Peer pressure is a huge thing for not-yet-mature boys. It is part of the growing and development process. Boys also look to their peers for acceptance and approval. However, let him know that he should trust himself and, that the more he knows and understands himself, the happier he will be. He should rely on *his* assessment of himself, and that assessment should be based on reality. His talents and abilities are just that. They do not reflect on him as a person. In a race he might be slower than some boys and faster than others. So long as he feels he is doing his best, that's all that matters. And there will also be times when he doesn't feel like doing his best. And that's okay too.

Contemporary life, including social media and the internet generally, these days, seems to encourage a form of narcissism, a solipsistic self-obsession.

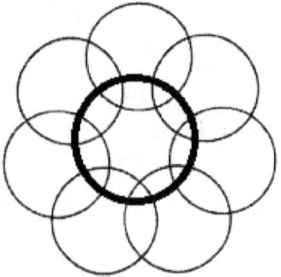

I remember, when I was about eight years old, suddenly realizing that the whole world didn't just revolve around me.

That my 'circle' overlapped and interlocked with other peoples' 'circles', and that each person had their own 'circle'. It was quite a revelation to me. I became interested in other people and their lives. This, in turn, helped me to develop a greater sense of compassion. And this is also the sort of way of approaching life that you might discuss with your son. It will make him stronger as a man, more realized as a god and, in fact, help him to fit in better into the world. It will also help him to have more compassion for himself.

All of your son's physical characteristics are also just that, whether he is short, tall, fat, or thin. He could possibly be his own worst critic and may compare himself to other boys. But if you can help him to accept himself in all areas, that will stand him in good stead for the rest of his life.

Discuss shame and guilt with your son. Gently try and find out whether he is prone to either. If he is, find a way to dissuade him from them Obviously you are not going to say to him "You're an idiot if you feel guilty". But you can explain what a waste of energy they both are. Also beware of *you* imposing either shame or guilt on him. Fathers sometimes do this either as a method of control over their sons or because that's what was done to them as boys.

Some of the best things that you can do for your son are to show him your own god-ness. Demonstrate what it's like to be a god. Remember you're not replacing God in his eyes (in fact there can sometimes be a tendency for small boys to regard their fathers as God), but you are just being fully *you*. Also you can help him by being there for him. That includes paying attention to him and listening to him. Learn about *him*. It also means interacting with him and sharing with him as much as you can about yourself.

Ensure that you teach your son to honour and respect women, starting with his mother. Obviously the best way to do this is by example: in how *you* interact with all women. And don't forget it's also how you talk about women when they're not present. Your son will follow your lead.

Be alert too to how he behaves with women and girls and how he talks about them when not in their presence.

Instill in your son that women are entitled to equality of opportunity in all respects, Women are not inferior or superior to men, they are our complementary other half - the Divine Feminine to our Divine Masculine. And that men and women can learn from one another.

Just as you may have found the concept that you are a god difficult to believe, so too might your son may find it difficult to grasp or accept that he is also a god. He may simply reject that possibility. Naturally you would listen to the reasons why it's hard for him to accept. Then, rather than simply rebutting those reasons, work with him to try and find out what *his* reasons are. They may or may not be the same as yours. If he simply can't accept the premise, first re-phrase it, that it's simply about being the best he can be. And use the elite sportsman analogy. Ultimately, if he's just not interested, don't push him. He can come to it in his own time. It won't stop you from edifying him. Whatever you do, don't impose your beliefs on him, Allow him to make up his own mind.

Similarly, help him to *keep* remembering that he is a god. NOT by nagging, but gently in subtle ways. Remember, it's about encouraging him. Use all of your empathy in this area and try to remember what it was like for you at his age. Use all the cues and keys that you've learned to remember.

Encourage your son in his mindfulness, starting with meditation. Show him your practice and let him experiment with that and other practices. Allow him to find his own path in this area at his own pace. Certainly do not push him, but guide him gently. If he is not receptive to your guidance, then drop it and perhaps mention it at a later date. On the other hand, ensure that you do impress upon him the importance of mindfulness. It can help him in all areas, including his schoolwork.

Have a discussion with him about any conversations that he might have with his friends about being a god. I'm sure that you want to protect him as much as you are able, and there is, of course, the possibility that he could be ridiculed by his friends. On the other hand, ensure that he knows that you are not talking about it being a secret. Simply that others might not understand. Make it clear too that others might confuse him being a god with claiming that he is God, and they might be offended by that claim.

The bottom line is that this is a delicate subject. By keeping certain knowledge 'secret' that is the way that religions and secret societies are born. And that's NOT what we're talking about at all!

And, at the end of the day, you may feel that it is better not to mention the word 'god' until he is older and, to your best ability, simply guide him along the path

There is an excellent chance that your son will be rebellious at some stage and that he might reject all of your guidance as far as this subject (and just about any subject) is concerned. Mark Twain is quoted as saying: "When I was a boy of 14, my father was so ignorant I could hardly stand to have the old man around. But when I got to be 21, I was astonished at how much the old man had learned in seven years." So, while you're helping your son throughout that period, be careful not to push him about being a god. Let him come to it in his own time.

MARTIN GUINNESS

And....if none of the above works for you and/or him, at least point him to the Rudyard Kipling poem "If", and ensure that he reads it repeatedly "

If you can keep your head when all about you
    Are losing theirs and blaming it on you,
If you can trust yourself when all men doubt you,
    But make allowance for their doubting too;
If you can wait and not be tired by waiting,
    Or being lied about, don't deal in lies,
Or being hated, don't give way to hating,
    And yet don't look too good, nor talk too wise:

If you can dream—and not make dreams your master;
    If you can think—and not make thoughts your aim;
If you can meet with Triumph and Disaster
    And treat those two impostors just the same;
If you can bear to hear the truth you've spoken
    Twisted by knaves to make a trap for fools,
Or watch the things you gave your life to, broken,
    And stoop and build 'em up with worn-out tools:

If you can make one heap of all your winnings
    And risk it on one turn of pitch-and-toss,
And lose, and start again at your beginnings
    And never breathe a word about your loss;
If you can force your heart and nerve and sinew
    To serve your turn long after they are gone,
And so hold on when there is nothing in you
    Except the Will which says to them: 'Hold on!'

If you can talk with crowds and keep your virtue,
    Or walk with Kings—nor lose the common touch,

THE GOD THAT YOU ARE

If neither foes nor loving friends can hurt you,
  If all men count with you, but none too much;
If you can fill the unforgiving minute
  With sixty seconds' worth of distance run,
Yours is the Earth and everything that's in it,
  And—which is more—you'll be a Man, my son!

And…more than that, he will also be the god that he is.

17: LIVE AS A GOD

> **'Through living your life to its fullest you can ascertain *your* truth.'**

As a god you have responsibilities. You have a responsibility for yourself and your dependants. You are also responsible to your culture, your society, and your country. And you are responsible for this planet. All of these responsibilities need to be balanced against one another. Just as you would not (I hope) feed yourself and totally disregard your children, being a god and caring for yourself does not mean disregarding everybody and everything else. Part of being a god is also to open your heart and to expand your altruism, your unselfish concern for others. This is the very essence of a true society with healthy members of that society.

At its very core, this book is about your potential and realizing that potential. In the process it's also about self-empowerment. However, it's essential to not just consider yourself. It's also about society as a whole.

Mahatma Gandhi said "If we could change ourselves, the tendencies in the world would also change. As a man changes his own nature, so does the attitude of the world change towards him. This is the divine mystery supreme. A wonderful thing it is and the source of our happiness. We need not wait to see what others do."

If all men could reach their full potential as gods (and all women reach their full potential as goddesses), then who knows how far civilization might develop. There is a frequently-asked question, "Why are we here?", and I happen to believe that the very reason that we're here is for mankind to develop to its absolute utmost – to reach its zenith. But, effectively, we can only go as fast as the slowest member of society.

So I believe that we need to develop ourselves as individuals, but also that we need to encourage others to develop. My life is totally dedicated to that principle right now, and is, of course, the reason for me writing this book. I would like you to fully develop as a god and then to assist in helping other men to develop as gods. Can you imagine the energy – the force – if we can make that happen; what we might do as a group of fully-realized individuals.

I've already briefly touched on the dangers of creating a religion. Goodness knows the world doesn't need any more Organized Religions! But I'm not talking about creating a religion. I'm talking about us unifying with each other and becoming one with existence.

Wisdom

There is a tendency today for people to simply throw facts at one another. This is done unthinkingly in a sheep-like fashion as though these facts are a substitute for original thought and wisdom. Social media has only made this situation worse. But, here's the thing: While facts, information and knowledge are important:

> Facts are **not** information
> Information is **not** knowledge
> Knowledge is **not** wisdom

We need to stop communicating with each other just using facts or data. They have their place. But far more important for us is to develop wisdom: both individual and collective wisdom. Wisdom is very thin on the ground right now and very hard to find.

Those organizations which seem to have our best interests at heart in fact seem to be driven by self-interest or by the profit-motive. For example, we have learned not to trust banks, the mass media and the corporate world, Our politicians have generally failed us and so have our priests. So it is up to us as individuals to firstly develop our own wisdom and then to share it with others.

Wisdom is a form of intelligence. Not an intellectual intelligence that utilizes the brain, but a native intelligence that calls on all of our senses. It can be learned and it can be developed. And sometimes it's innate in us. Some men learn wisdom from their parents or teachers. Some men go out in search of opportunities to develop their wisdom. And all gods welcome those opportunities.

I urge you to develop your own wisdom. Through your journey of self-discovery your general level of awareness can be increased. Through living your life to its fullest you can ascertain *your* truth. Through learning you can increase your knowledge. And, while knowledge is not wisdom, it can lead to wisdom. However, there are additional qualities that you will require in order to become wiser. The first is humility. Socrates, the Greek philosopher, said "As for me, all I know is that I know nothing". That is a very good place from which to start. If you begin with the premise that you are a blank page for wisdom to be written upon, you will be heading in the right direction.

Learn to 'read' people. This does not mean pigeon-holing them or pre-judging them. It means looking for what gamblers call a 'tell', a way that they behave, the tone of their voice, their body language, their breathing. Study people that you know and, without any judgment or criticism, simply notice what's happening with them. Look out for consistencies and inconsistencies, and notice how they match up with events. These are subtle signals, and you will have to pay close attention. It is a skill that is possible to learn. Through it you will increase one aspect of perception, which is a major element of wisdom. Perception is defined as the process of recognizing and interpreting sensory stimuli. But remember your 'sixth' sense – your intuition. The better your sense of intuition, the more chance you have of increasing your wisdom.

Learn to anticipate people and situations. Study people and their methods and timing of doing things and do your best to read situations before they occur. This takes focus, awareness and experience, but it will assist you in many ways.

Study the nature of things to sense the energetic currents that cause events to happen and, in turn, the repercussions of those events.

Try and understand your own and other peoples' motivations: what would make them behave in a particular way; why they would respond/react in a particular way; is there fear, need, desire, behind their actions and what they say? Do not take others' actions personally. Learn to look below the surface. What they say or do is *their* thing. Try to listen to what they're *really* saying and observe what they're *really* doing. It's possible that they're trying to convey something entirely different from what you perceive.

Maintaining an open mind in all matters will definitely assist you. When I was younger I knew someone who would joke "I've made up my mind, don't confuse me with the facts". He was joking, but

THE GOD THAT YOU ARE

what he was saying was accurate. He had *always* made up his mind. And he always had an opinion about *everything*. Each situation is always different, just as each person is different (and, actually, people are always changing anyway). There is a huge difference between being aware of your previous experience and making assumptions in the moment. Having preconceived ideas will inhibit your ability to dance with each person and each situation as it arises. How could your wisdom stand a chance in that situation?

Don't be small-minded. Be generous in all things. Be especially generous in giving yourself to other people. By this I mean make your *self* available. Knock down those invisible barriers between you and others. As a god you have a huge amount to offer to others. Don't be stingy with that energy. Show people by word and deed how a god can be. Speak the truth. Be real and authentic and a solid, reliable man. Be clear with your and others' boundaries. When you interact with others have the courage to not be afraid of consequences such as retribution by others. And, remember, your beliefs are *your* beliefs. You can *not* impose them on others.

Knowing yourself is another initial step to gaining wisdom. Which is why there is so much emphasis in this book on gaining knowledge about yourself. If you can see how you act (and, especially, how you *re*act), and then understand why you have acted in that way, you will begin to know yourself. Similarly, if you can understand why other people act and react the way that they do, it will be another step. Not only will these understandings bring you compassion for yourself and others, it will help you to gain perspective on human nature. It will also help you to see that all human beings have foibles and idiosyncrasies. Understanding that will also mean you will have less anticipation of them behaving according to your expectations. On the other hand, by observing people over a period of time you will come to understand how they *might* behave in any given situation.

However, wisdom takes in more than just understanding the ways of people. It also includes a real appreciation that there are certain forces (natural laws) at play in the world in which we live. For example, Isaac Newton's Third Law states that "For every action, there is an equal and opposite reaction". You can see this happen physically: for example, think of a pendulum. It will swing away from the midpoint and will then overcorrect itself as it returns. This effect (and the law that governs it) also occurs in our world where it is difficult to observe with our physical senses. We must 'sense' it with another part of ourselves. This 'sensing' is part of what forms what we call 'wisdom', and is the understanding of how things 'work' in our world.

This energy also works with the natural elements of our planet — for example, the oceans and the winds. And it is also occurs on a much more subtle and abstruse level. In other words, there are forces at play with which most people only experience the outcomes, not the forces themselves. But, if you can be at least aware that these forces exist, and also be aware when they're taking place, then you can begin to develop wisdom.

Some of wisdom is simply common sense. That is, it is sound, practical and objective judgment that is free of subjective interpretation and reactive thought and behaviour. That sounds easy, doesn't it? But a great deal seems to happen in the world where common sense appears to be entirely absent.

Wisdom is also, in part having discernment or good judgment. By which I mean judgment of a situation rather than a person. I have never yet met or heard of anyone who has never made a mistake or who has always made good judgments. It is human to misjudge a situation. In fact the 'trial & error' process is part of our growth as men, and certainly as gods. Every time you make a 'mistake' you will have learned something. And you can put all those 'mistakes' together with all your 'successes' to help build your ability to assess future situations. The points are: firstly, to minimize any poor judgments; and secondly, to learn from them. Each time you do that you will sharpen your ability to distinguish what is 'right' for you and what is 'wrong'. Of course, having your open mind, this might change over time. But it is right in that moment. And, if it becomes consistently right, that will develop into natural discernment.

Experience is the biggest teacher of wisdom that you can have. Therefore, naturally, the older you become, the wiser you should be. Unfortunately that doesn't always happen. So the more experiences that you can have, the more opportunities there will be to teach you wisdom. Immerse yourself in as much as possible. Meet as many people (and, especially, as many *types* of people) as possible. Involve yourself in as many different types of activity as possible.

As I've mentioned before, travel will also teach you many things. And spending longer periods of time in different countries and cultures will give you a different sense of perspective. In my life I have lived in four different countries across three continents. This has broadened my knowledge, but it's also given me a greater sense of understanding.

Constantly refining your wisdom and understanding will form an essential part of you being a god. Learn to trust your own wisdom

Happiness

A major part of living as a god is allowing yourself to be happy as much as possible. Yes, "allowing". Why do I say that? Because men often swing between 'trying' to be happy and preventing themselves from actually being happy. Some people have a subconscious belief that they don't deserve happiness. Be clear with yourself. Is that true for you on any level? If you discover that it is true for you, the next question is why do you hold that belief? It may well be deeply ingrained in you. In other words, you were told it or you learned by patterning from others when you were a child. Alternatively, you might feel shame or guilt about something in your life. If any of these are true I strongly urge you to look deeply at them and work with these subconscious (or, in some cases, conscious) thoughts so that you can allow yourself to be happy. Working with a professional counsellor can often help you with this.

In my experience it's extremely difficult to *make* yourself happy. Of course you can involve yourself in all kinds of activities and do all sorts of things where, in the past, happiness has occurred. Naturally you know the optimal situations where you might be happy. But it doesn't always work, does it? Why is that, do you suppose? It's because happiness is a passive state of being. For example, you might suddenly stop and realize that you feel happy. And the experience might be transitory or it might last over an extended period of time. However, the point is that what's happening in the process is that you're letting go of all the things that actually prevent you from being happy and simply allowing it to happen. And, as a god, you can do that more and more frequently.

There is a greater chance of happiness when your energy is flowing, when you feel free, and when your mind is not caught up in obsessive thoughts. Being able to truly feel gratitude will also bring happiness. If you can 'count your blessings' on a regular basis you will have a better chance of being happy.

Be sure to pat yourself on your own back when you complete something or achieve something. Celebrate your accomplishments. Self-congratulation is not a sin.

Happiness is infectious. Sharing your happiness with others will help them, and vice versa is also true.

And, eventually, it becomes a way of life. So much so, that you can go beyond happiness to bliss. This is the ultimate state for a god.

The Danish word Hygge (pronounced "hooga") roughly translates as creating a sense of wellbeing in yourself and others in order to be happy and is a tradition in Denmark. A major way to manifest hygge is by creating a warm atmosphere and enjoying the good things in life. The warm glow of candlelight in cosy surroundings is hygge. Sharing and celebrating happiness with friends and family is especially important in developing providing a setting for your happiness to occur.

I wonder whether you've been on holiday to somewhere new. As you walk around the unfamiliar streets you can experience a sense of wonder and delight at the various sights. What I do sometimes is to walk around the streets of my own neighbourhood and try to see everything through the eyes of a holiday-maker as though for the first time, so that I really see the details of everything and can take pleasure in them. This pleasure becomes happiness in me.

Personal Growth

What does personal growth mean to you? For me it feels like life itself. I was going to say that it also feels like I have no choice. But I was asking myself recently "Do I have a choice?". Could I just go "Okay, that's it. I've grown as much as I need to. Now I'll just rest on my laurels". I certainly know quite a few people who've done that. And good luck to them. But there's something inside of me that needs that continual expansion. I feel that, like a tree, once

I stop growing, I'll die. Of course, along the way unneeded bits will drop off (and other less-than-useful parts may be lopped of – sometimes painfully); I'll flower at different times; and I'll be dormant at others - as I take time to take stock and re-establish who I am. So, really, I seem to have about as much choice as that tree. I imagine that I'll just keep growing right up to the point that I actually do die.

Wear your god-ness out in the world. But there is absolutely no need to go around proclaiming that you are a god. When you believe it for yourself – when you can *be* a god – the whole world will notice and behave towards you accordingly. They will not need to be told.

And, finally…

Find *your* truth (not somebody else's – including mine). Be clear who you are and what you think.

Remember: it's not that you have to *change* into something that you are not. It's that you can just *be* what you already are. Let's be clear about this: You were born to be a god. It is your birthright. And you should settle for nothing less. Live the fullest version of your highest self,

The American metaphysician Neville Goddard said "You are already that which you want to be, and your refusal to believe it is the only reason you do not see it"

I hope you have enjoyed this book and found it useful. If so, please tell other people about it.

Thank you.

Martin Guinness.

APPENDIX

A little exercise to practise projecting your energy:

Here's an exercise you can try anytime you're with other people. Start by imagining your skin inside your clothing. Bring your attention to each part of your body in turn. Now imagine very gentle currents of air moving around your head and face. Take your time and breathe gently. Feel the wholeness of your being. This is you as a physical entity: One complete individual being. When you're ready, start to feel what's on the 'other side' of your being: where you meet the outside world. Get a sense of that edge.

As you continue to breathe gently imagine extending that edge just a little all around you, so that your body is one centimetre bigger all around, including being a little taller. Feel comfortable in that space.

Now, whether you're sitting by yourself or you're interacting with other people, you can continue to expand your energy so that it overflows and not just meets other people's energy, but actually envelopes them.

You can continue to be your authentic self as you talk, laugh, and generally interact with others.

The 'light bulb' meditation:

This is another little exercise that you can do in order to be in balance and harmony with yourself and the world. Unusually, it's a meditation that is best done standing up (although you can do it any way you choose).

Stand with your legs a little apart and your knees unlocked. Rock gently on your feet, so that you can feel your connection to the ground beneath you.

Hold out both arms, elbows relaxed, with the palms of your hands facing upwards.

Now think about a light bulb: how power comes from a source, passes through the light bulb, and then passes back towards the source. What it has done along the way is to fill the light bulb with energy – infusing it with light and warmth.

You are going to be that light bulb. Feel the power enter your body through your left palm. This power is infinite and abundant. Feel the energy circulate throughout your whole body, filling up your entire being and bringing strength, power and light to your soul and every part of you as it passes out of you through your right palm. Allow the power to continue circulating in this way for as long as you choose.

The tense-relax exercise:

Whether you are feeling really stressed, you just want to relax, or you want to clear your head, this exercise is very useful.

Find a quiet space to lie down, preferably away from other people and distractions. You might like to turn the lights down and possibly put on some very quiet music.

Allow your eyes to close

Bring your attention to the toes on your left foot. Then breath in as you curl your toes. Hold the toes curled and your breath. Hold the tension and your breath for a few seconds. Then slowly breathe out as you release the tension.

Next try and tense the muscles around your left ankle as you inhale. And, again, hold the tension and your breath for a few seconds. Then slowly breathe out as you release the tension.

Repeat this with your calf, knee and thigh muscles,

Then repeat all this with your right leg.

Start to work your way up the body. In each case inhaling as you tense. Holding both. Then exhaling as you release the tension.

Bring your energy to your groin, your hips, your stomach, and your chest, and tense-relax your muscles and hold-release your breath.

Feel the fingers on your left hand and repeat the action. Then all the muscles in your left arm.

Then repeat it all again with your right arm.

Tense your neck muscles, and all your facial muscles in turn, repeating the tension and relaxation.

Now feel the muscles on the very top of your head and do the same.

And finally try and tense all the muscles in your body and head as you hold your breath for as long as possible. When you can't hold it any longer, release your breath and the tension as slowly as possible.

Stay lying down for a few minutes, enjoying the feeling of relaxation.

When you're ready, allow your eyes to open, and gently stretch your body

www.ingramcontent.com/pod-product-compliance
Lightning Source LLC
Chambersburg PA
CBHW071918290426
44110CB00013B/1405